KU-215-757

The Hardy Boys®
in
The Masked Monkey

This Armada book belongs to:

_____

_____

_____

Hardy Boys® Mystery Stories in Armada

For contractual reasons, Armada has been obliged to publish from No. 57 onwards before publishing Nos. 45–56. These missing numbers will be published as soon as possible.

The Hardy Boys® Mystery Stories

The Masked Monkey

Franklin W. Dixon

Armada

First published in the U.K. in 1979 by
William Collins Sons & Co. Ltd, London and Glasgow
First published in Armada in 1987

Armada is an imprint of
the Children's Division, part of
the Collins Publishing Group,
8 Grafton Street, London W1X 3LA

Printed in Great Britain by
William Collins Sons & Co. Ltd, Glasgow

Contents

Frank met the first attacker with a stiff right-hand punch.

The Hardy Boys® Mystery Stories

The Masked Monkey

·1·

A Puzzling Disappearance

"YOU mean your eighteen-year-old son drew fifty thousand dollars from his bank account and then disappeared?" dark-haired Frank Hardy asked incredulously. His blond brother Joe, sitting beside him on a sofa, also looked bewildered.

The two teenage investigators from Bayport were in the posh office of J. G. Retson, owner of a stone quarry near Granite City. He sat behind his desk, rocking nervously in a high-backed chair.

"Yes!" Retson answered Frank's question. "That's exactly what I mean. The fifty grand is gone, and so is Graham."

"And you want us to find him?"

"That's right!" Retson declared, striking the desk with his fist. "Find him and bring him back home. Tell him he can be anything he wants to be. He has my word on that."

"Sounds as if there's been a family quarrel," Joe observed.

Retson threw his hands in the air with a pained expression. "Graham and I didn't understand each other as a father and son should," he confessed. "He had some weird ideas I didn't go along with. But things will be different when he gets home. I won't try to change him any more."

The industrialist paused. All choked up, he pulled a handkerchief from his breast pocket and dabbed his eyes.

The Hardy boys felt embarrassed. They waited silently until Retson regained his composure.

"We'll do our best," Joe assured him. "But we'll need some clues. How long has Graham been missing?"

Retson folded his handkerchief and replaced it in his pocket. "Two months," he replied.

"You must have made some effort to find him in that time," Frank said.

"Of course. I went to the Granite City police when he didn't come home after a few days."

"Any results?" Joe asked.

"Nothing. Every lead petered out. Chief Carton calls it the most baffling case he's ever worked on. And he's cracked some big ones."

Frank stared out the window while he puzzled over the mysterious disappearance of Graham Retson. Then he remarked, "Sir, you obviously think we might succeed where the police failed. Why us?"

"I know your reputation as detectives," Retson replied. "According to the papers, you've helped your father on many of his cases."

Retson was referring to Fenton Hardy, the renowned detective, who had been a member of the New York City police force before becoming a private investigator. Frank, eighteen years old, and Joe, a year younger, were well experienced in tracking down criminals. Their first case was *The Mystery of the Aztec Warrior*, and their latest success, *The Bombay Boomerang*. But this seemed to be a different kind of mystery.

Retson continued. "That's not all. The point is, you're both about my son's age. There's a generation gap between Graham and me. But you fellows speak his lingo. You should be able to get through to him."

"We'll try," Frank said, "if we can find him."

Retson gave a deep sigh. "That's a relief. Stay right with the case. Money is no object. Spend whatever it takes. Go to the ends of the earth if you must, but find my son!"

"We'll give it all we've got," Joe vowed. "But we'll need some information from you."

"Such as?"

"Photos, letters, diary—anything that might give us a lead."

"I see what you mean," Retson said. "Well, I'll give you all the help I can. Come out to my place, Whisperwood, tomorrow. It's on a ridge of Granite Rock near the waterfall. Take the highway west till you see the wire fence round the property. You can examine Graham's personal belongings."

"We'll be there." Frank and Joe left the office, climbed into their convertible, and headed back to Bayport.

"What do you think of it?" Frank asked as he turned the car into the driveway of their home.

"Let's discuss it with Dad tonight," Joe suggested.

"He won't be home until late. But we'll see him in the morning."

At breakfast the next day Mr Hardy listened closely while his sons described their visit to Granite City.

"It's a real mystery," he admitted. "No wonder Retson's worried."

"Dad, can you give us a hand?" Joe asked.

Fenton Hardy smiled but shook his head. "I'd like to, but I'm tied up with a fake passport case. A ring of unsavoury characters is doctoring stolen United States passports. Strange coincidence, they were stolen in Granite City in a post office holdup two years ago. So I'm off to Washington this morning."

As the front door closed behind him the phone rang. Joe answered, heard a familiar voice, and turned to Frank with a grin. "It's Chet," he said.

Chet Morton was the Hardy boys' best friend. A plump, freckle-faced youth who jolted round town in an ancient jalopy, he was always involved in some new hobby.

Frank chuckled. "What's he up to?"

Chet was telling Joe excitedly, "I want to see you guys right away. Got a big deal on! If you sweet-talk me, maybe I'll give you a piece of the action. I'm coming over to your house pronto."

"No use, Chet," Joe said. "We're on our way to a meeting in Granite City."

Chet gave a low whistle. "You're on another case? . . . Say, is there anything I can do? Nothing too dangerous, of course."

He had helped the Hardys solve several mysteries. Though Chet was not fond of hair-raising assignments, Frank and Joe knew they could rely on him when the going got rough.

"We've just started," Joe answered. "We'll know more when we get back tonight. Come on over tomorrow and we'll talk."

"Okay," Chet replied. "And we'll discuss my big deal, too."

"Right." Joe laughed. He hung up and joined Frank for the drive to Granite City.

Beyond the outskirts of Bayport, Frank swung the convertible on to the highway leading west. After two hours the level terrain gave way to a section of hills and ravines. The car rolled through a pass cut in solid rock.

"There's the ridge Mr Retson mentioned," said Joe, glancing ahead at Granite Rock. "And that must be the fence round Whisperwood." He pointed to a tall barrier of heavy meshed wire.

"Right, Joe. It's a huge estate. I don't even see the gate yet. Oh, there it is." Frank guided the car past a stand of pine trees and stopped before a large iron portal guarding the entrance. A brass bell was mounted beside it.

Joe got out and tried to turn the massive handle. "Locked," he muttered. "And there's not a sign of a gatekeeper to let us inside this fortress."

Frank jangled the bell clapper, and the sound boomed through the grounds, but it brought no response. "Looks as if they don't want company," he muttered.

"Well, we've got an invitation," Joe said. "It's not polite for a couple of guests to keep their host waiting. So here goes."

Grasping the fence wire with his fingers, Joe got a toehold and climbed up the fence. He dropped down on the other side to the sound of tearing cloth.

"Ripped my jacket," he groaned. "Well, I made it, though. Come on."

Frank, who had followed Joe up the fence, jumped down. Together they walked towards the Whisperwood mansion, outlined against the sky at the summit of the ridge. A butler answered the bell.

"My name is Harris," he announced in solemn tones. "Mr Retson is expecting you. But you've torn your jacket, Mr Hardy. Here, let me have it and I'll see it's repaired before you leave. I'm so sorry I didn't hear the bell clapper."

Joe handed over the garment, then the butler ushered them into Retson's den.

Their client apologized when he heard about their experience at the gate. "I didn't expect you so early. You see, I do insist on complete privacy in Whisperwood."

"Think nothing of it, Mr Retson," Frank said. "Let's get down to the question of where your son might be. First of all, what does he look like?"

Retson lifted a photograph from the mantelpiece. "This was taken a few days before Graham disappeared."

Frank and Joe examined the picture. They saw a frail youth wearing long hair and glasses with round metal rims that made him appear owlish.

"Any distinguishing characteristics, Mr Retson?" Frank asked.

"Yes. Graham has a nervous habit of nodding his head while he's talking."

Joe looked hard at the photo. "He's not the rugged type, if I'm any judge."

"Hardly. Graham is very sensitive. In fact, he spends most of his time writing poetry."

"What started the feud between you two?" Joe wanted to know.

Retson snorted. "A cage of silly hamsters. Graham

brought the beasts home. I stood them as long as I could. Then one day when my son was out, I told the butler to get rid of them."

"Could we have a look at Graham's poetry?" Frank asked.

Retson opened a cabinet and pulled out a magazine. "Here, this is published by the private school he went to. You'll find his stuff on page 58. It's all Greek to me."

Frank spread the magazine on top of the cabinet. The boys began to read the verses.

"Say, this isn't bad," Frank said. "Your son has talent."

"But it doesn't tell us where he is," Joe mused. "We'd better have a look at his room."

Retson led the way up a broad staircase to a bedroom at the end of the hall. "I hope you'll find a clue here to Graham's whereabouts," he remarked, and left them.

The Hardys searched the closets, carefully looked through the bureau drawers, and examined the missing youth's collection of poetry books.

Joe was disappointed. "I haven't found anything here."

"Let's try the desk," Frank said.

They went through the drawers, beginning at the top centre, working down the left side and then turning to the right.

"Still nothing," Joe said. "No diary, no letters, no clues."

He started to slam the bottom drawer shut when Frank grabbed his arm.

"Wait a minute, Joe. What's this?" Frank reached to the back of the drawer and pulled out a crumpled piece of paper. Unfolding it, he read aloud four lines of verse:

> " 'My life is a walled city
>   From which I must flee;
> This must my prison be
>   So long as I am me.' "

Frank turned the paper over. There were two more lines on the other side.

> " 'There is a way,
>   But what it is I cannot say.' "

Joe said, "This could be a clue! Judging by those first four lines, Graham wasn't too happy here."

"And the last two lines could mean he found a way to escape," Frank said.

Just then Mr Retson came into the room. Frank showed him the piece of paper. "Is this Graham's handwriting?" he asked.

"Yes."

"May we keep it? It might be a message in code."

"Certainly. Keep anything that will help you find Graham. Incidentally, you can stay at Whisperwood while you're on the case. There's an apartment over the old stable. The horses are gone, so we've had the rooms renovated and call it the guesthouse."

Frank and Joe decided they might accept the offer later on.

"We'd better get back to Bayport today," Joe said. "If we find it would be easier working from here, we'll be glad to park ourselves over the stable."

The butler showed the visitors out. "Here's your

jacket, Mr Hardy," he said to Joe. "I believe you will find the repairs satisfactory."

"Looks as good as new," Joe assured him. "Thanks a lot."

When the young detectives arrived home, Joe hung his jacket in the hall closet. Something crinkled in one pocket. He reached in and pulled out a folded page torn from a small notebook.

"What's that?" Frank queried.

"A bit of scribbling. Apparently somebody wrote it in a hurry."

"What does it say?"

Joe read, " 'Don't look for Graham. You'll ruin his life!' "

·2·

Bouncing Balls

"THIS is a warning!" Frank gasped. "Who could have written it, Joe?"

"Harris the butler could have slipped the paper into the pocket before returning my jacket."

"We'd better have a talk with Harris," Frank declared. "If he's trying to scare us off the case, I'd like to know the reason."

"You boys are jumping to conclusions," said a tart voice behind them. Fenton Hardy's sister was dusting the living room. Gertrude Hardy lived with her brother and his family. She loved her nephews dearly. But she never hesitated to give her opinion about the boys' detective work.

"I heard what you said about the butler," she went on, flicking her duster around a vase. "And I say you're jumping to conclusions. I've read enough murder mysteries to know that the butler is always accused."

"We're not accusing him, Aunty," Frank said. "He just seems to be the prime suspect at this point. Anyway, this isn't a murder mystery. At least we don't know that anybody's been murdered."

"We're involved in a missing-person case," Joe explained. "Graham Retson lived at Whisperwood near

18

Granite City with his parents. He's disappeared under mysterious circumstances."

"Granite City!" Miss Hardy sniffed. "That's a hundred miles from here. You'll burn a lot of fuel commuting back and forth!"

"Not necessarily," Joe replied. "Mr Retson offered to put us up at Whisperwood over his stable while we're hunting for clues. Besides, there might not be a criminal involved at all."

Gertrude Hardy clucked like a broody hen. "Stable indeed! Mr Retson should have offered you better lodgings. One of you might get kicked by a horse."

Frank and Joe soothed their aunt by assuring her there were no horses at Whisperwood to do any kicking.

"Well, I imagine you'll find some kind of danger there," Aunt Gertrude said. "So be careful." With this parting shot, she flounced out of the room.

Frank and Joe mulled over the strange disappearance of Graham Retson and the warning note. They decided to accept the industrialist's offer and go to Whisperwood the next day.

In the morning Frank and Joe were having breakfast with their mother and Aunt Gertrude when a series of rackety explosions erupted in the street.

"That's Chet's jalopy," Laura Hardy said.

The doorbell rang and Frank let their friend in. He was puffing with excitement as he entered the dining room.

"Morning, Mrs Hardy, Aunt Gertrude," he said. When he saw the food on the table, he halted in delight, rubbed his belt buckle, and glanced significantly at the women.

"Chester Morton, there's no mystery about what

you want," said Gertrude Hardy. "Can I tempt you with some pancakes?"

"Please do," replied Chet, who loved nothing better than eating.

Joe laughed. "After all, our buddy's only had one breakfast this morning. His inner man is telling him it's time for an encore."

Chet sat down and consumed a stack of pancakes at an alarming rate. He also drank two glasses of milk. Then he leaned back with a pleased expression. "That was just great," he said as the women cleared the table. "Thanks very much."

"Okay," Joe said. "What's the big deal you mentioned on the phone yesterday?"

Chet rolled his eyes. "You guys ever heard of golf ball scavenging?"

"Negative," Frank said. "What is it? A new hobby?"

"No, a get-rich-quick scheme. Duffers keep dunking golf balls in water hazards on most of the golf courses. Scavengers retrieve them and sell them. I'm a scavenger, and I'll cut you in if you're interested."

"We might be," Frank said, "when we have the time."

"We've got to go back to Granite City this afternoon," Joe told Chet.

"You can't do that!" Chet protested. "I'm counting on you. Hold everything. You've got this morning free, right?"

Frank and Joe nodded.

"Okay," Chet went on. "That's enough time to start operations. Let's go."

The three climbed into Chet's jalopy and drove to the farm outside of Bayport where he lived. On the way,

Chet explained how golf balls were retrieved.

"Many amateur divers and frogmen," he said, "descend into water hazards to scour the bottom. Professionals, however, don't go into the water. They use suction pumps and underwater vacuum cleaners.

"About sixty million balls are recovered every year," Chet stated, "and are resold for about fifteen million dollars."

Frank whistled. "That's a lot of money."

"Enough to buy several golf courses," Joe remarked.

"Sure," Chet said. "And I aim to get my share of the dough from the golf courses around Bayport."

At the Morton farm the three transferred to a small truck. In the back was a very large box with a petrol engine attached. Lines of small holes showed on one side, and a long hose dangled from one corner.

"Dad's letting me use his pick-up truck," Chet said. "I spent a week building the retriever. Come on. Let's go to the nearest course and see how my suction pump works."

When they arrived at the Bayport links, Chet explained his gadget to the club's golf pro. He was willing to let the boys have a try at the water hazard, providing they gave him half the golf balls they recovered.

The trio then drove to a pond at the third hole. Chet turned on the engine, pushed the nozzle of the hose down through the water, and began to vacuum the bottom.

A mixture of mud and water, sucked through the hose into the container, spewed out through the side holes and back into the pond. Loud rattling came from inside.

"Those are the golf balls!" Chet exulted. "They're

too big to go through the holes, so they're banging against the sides. We've struck it rich!"

"The pump works like a charm," Joe admitted. "Chet, for once you've come up with something practical."

About an hour later the pro rode up in a golf cart. He told them the recovery operation would have to wait until early evening because some golfers were impatient to play the third hole.

Chet wound up the hose and opened a door at the top of the container. Frank and Joe peered in. Several hundred golf balls—dirty and muddy from their stay in the pond, but otherwise in good condition—were piled up inside.

"We can sell these for a good profit," Chet said, "when we've cleaned them." After turning over half of the take to the golf pro, the boys tossed the rest into the back of the pick-up to dry off, and drove to Bayport.

As they went through the main intersection, a wild uproar broke out behind them. Horns blew. People shouted.

"What's wrong?" Chet muttered. "I didn't go through a stoplight!"

Joe, looking back, cried out, "We're paving the avenue with golf balls! The tailgate's open. We're losing them!"

Their cargo was streaming out of the pick-up into the crossing. Pedestrians went into frantic contortions as the golf balls rolled under their feet. Cars jolted to a halt. Traffic was snarled in four directions.

Chet pulled over to the kerb. "We're in for it now," he groaned.

"You can say that again," Frank muttered. "Here

comes the traffic cop. He looks pretty mad."

"And he's not too happy about running the obstacle course we just set up," Joe added.

"Everybody out!" the officer commanded the three youths. "Start picking them up!"

Frank, Joe, and Chet meekly climbed out of the truck and began gathering the golf balls. A group of youngsters pitched in for the fun of it. When the balls were back in the truck, Chet double-checked the tailgate before driving off.

"Lucky I didn't get a ticket," he sighed.

"And fortunately nobody got hurt," Frank said.

They arrived at the Hardy house to find their pals Phil Cohen and Tony Prito waiting for them. Phil was the sensitive, studious type, but could be counted on when Frank and Joe were on a dangerous mission.

Olive-skinned Tony, the son of a Bayport contractor, was another friend who frequently helped the Hardys solve mysteries.

The two were told about Chet's new business. They agreed to accompany him to the golf course that evening to complete the ball scavenging operation.

Frank and Joe drove to Whisperwood. They had dinner in a roadside restaurant. When they reached the estate, Retson showed them to his guesthouse. From a distance came a constant hissing sound.

"It's the waterfall," Retson explained. "It seems to be whispering all the time. That's why we called our home Whisperwood."

"Did your son ever come to the guesthouse?" Frank inquired.

"Yes, occasionally. You see, Harris used the place while a wing of the mansion was being renovated.

Graham liked him and visited him sometimes. Now the work on the house is done and Harris is back in his own quarters."

Joe described the incident of the note in his jacket pocket. "We'd like to talk to the butler about it," he said.

"Of course!" Retson replied. "Harris will have to answer to me if he's the one responsible."

Their host led the way back to the mansion, where they confronted the butler.

Joe handed the note to him. Harris became pale as he scrutinized the message. His eyes bulged. His breath came in gasps. He folded the note and handed it back. "Where did you find this?" he asked.

"In my jacket pocket, after you fixed it yesterday," Joe said.

Harris frowned. "If you think I wrote this, you are mistaken," he said.

"Can you prove that, Harris?" Retson asked harshly.

"Yes, indeed, sir. As you know, I make out the shopping list for the week. Here is the one I just wrote." Harris drew a sheet of paper from his pocket. "Compare my handwriting with the note Mr Hardy found in his coat."

Joe placed the two pieces of paper side by side. Frank looked on. The two scrawls obviously did not match!

"It seems someone else wrote the warning," Joe mused.

"But who?" Frank replied. "Who else lives in this house?"

"Jackson, the gardener," Retson said. "His wife is our cook. And of course there's Mrs Retson. My wife has had a nervous breakdown. She rarely leaves her room in the east wing. A nurse is on duty with her constantly. You can talk to Miss Hopkins if you want to. But don't bother Mrs Retson."

"We'll have to check out the whole staff," Frank said.

"Well, get on with the investigation first thing in the morning," Retson urged. "My son may have been kidnapped. Criminals may be holding him prisoner right now!"

Frank and Joe walked back to the guesthouse. "We're fresh out of clues," Joe commented.

"Maybe we'll come up with a theory after a little shut-eye," Frank said.

"That is, if we can get any shut-eye. Whisperwood gives me the willies. It's real spooky back here."

A high wind blew mournfully through the pines, and clouds scudded across the face of the moon. Granite Rock lay in deep shadows except for outcroppings of stone that resembled gigantic human figures trying to escape over the crest.

Despite the uncanny atmosphere, the boys fell into a deep sleep. They were awakened by a loud splintering sound in the middle of the night. A missile had crashed through the picture window into their room!

·3·

Careless Talk

"FRANK! What on earth was that?" Joe asked, fumbling for the light switch.

Frank had already jumped out of bed to the broken window. Bright moonlight gave him a clear view of the grounds. "No sign of the thrower," he reported. "Whoever it was ducked out of sight."

Joe turned on the small lamp next to his bed and the two searched around the room for the missile.

Joe reached under his bed. "Look," he said. "It's a golf ball!"

"I suppose it's a practical joke," Frank said. "But I don't think it's very funny."

"Whom do we know who might toss a golf ball in our direction?" Joe asked, raising an eyebrow.

"Chet Morton, that's who! Let's collar him if we can."

After dressing quickly, they hurried down the stairs and out the door. Joe circled the guest-house. Frank pushed through the bushes searching for a figure crouching behind them.

"When I spot an oversize shadow, that'll be our fun-loving pal," he said to himself.

Frank searched the bushes but found no one. Joe

reported failure too. Finally they returned to their room and slept soundly the rest of the night.

Early the next morning there was a knock on the door. Frank opened it. There stood Chet!

"Do come in," Frank invited. "We've been looking for you."

"Why?"

"What were you doing here last night?" Joe asked.

"What makes you think I was here?"

"This!" Joe showed him the golf ball. "It came through that window."

"Don't look at me," Chet protested. "I was home in Bayport!"

"You're here now," Frank put in.

"Sure. But I just arrived. I'm after golf ball scavenging contracts around Granite City. I just dropped by to see you two before making the rounds."

Frank shook his head. "You made a wonderful suspect. Now we're back where we started."

"Let me have a look at that ball," Chet said. He turned it over between his fingers. "Condor brand," he noted.

"Could find out where it came from?" Joe queried.

"Condors are popular," Chet said with an air of authority. "Even an expert such as myself might have trouble identifying a single ball. However, I'll ask around and see if any Granite City club sells Condors."

"How soon will you let us know?" Frank said.

"I'll stop by this evening and give you the info."

Chet drove off to the golf courses. Frank and Joe went to the Whisperwood mansion for breakfast, and told their host about the golf ball and the broken window at the guesthouse.

Retson also was puzzled, but finally he said, "I still suspect Harris."

"Why are you so down on your butler?" Frank inquired.

"Well, Graham spent a lot of time with Harris," Retson replied.

"More than with you?" Joe asked.

"Much more. I'd rather have seen the boy playing football. But no. He preferred writing verse. Harris said he liked the poetry, which could have been a come-on. He may well be part of a plot against my son."

The Hardys suggested checking the handwriting of the rest of the staff before accusing the butler. They set about gathering samples. Joe went to the kitchen, engaged the cook in conversation and persuaded her to write down a recipe for his mother.

Frank, buttonholing the gardener for a talk about the roses, managed to pocket a shopping list for seeds. Retson himself produced a memo written for Mrs Retson by Miss Hopkins, the nurse.

None of the samples of handwriting resembled that in the warning note found in Joe's jacket!

Frank looked disappointed. "We've learned what everybody's scrawl looks like, but that doesn't give us a lead."

"I still suspect Harris," Retson insisted.

"He could have had a confederate," Joe mused. "Maybe we should give him a lie detector test."

"I'll get him up here," Retson said. He pressed a button that rang a bell in the servants' quarters. The butler appeared.

Frank asked him, "Harris, you still claim to be innocent of that note, don't you?"

"Of course, Mr Hardy. I *am* innocent."

"Would you be willing to take a lie detector test to prove it?"

The butler blanched, but quickly regained control of himself. "Whenever you wish."

Joe offered to go to Granite City Police Headquarters and ask for a loan of a polygraph, the kind used in testing the veracity of suspects. He was back within the hour carrying a portable machine.

Harris sat patiently in a chair while the instruments for measuring pulse rate and blood pressure were attached to his body.

Frank set the graph which recorded physical reactions. Joe then directed a series of test questions at the butler. Then he said, "Harris, did you write that note I found in my jacket?"

"No."

"Do you know who wrote it?"

"No."

"Have you any idea where Graham is now?"

"No."

Watching the graph unroll, Frank saw that the pattern of the needle across the paper remained steady as the questioning continued. Finally he said, "Harris seems to be telling the truth."

Retson was clearly disappointed in the results of the test. He told the butler to leave the room and warned him to remain on the premises.

"I don't think he'll go anywhere," Frank said. "He seems like a loyal employee."

"Somebody here is disloyal!" Retson exclaimed. "How else do you explain away that note?"

Joe said, "You have to admit, Frank, it looks like an

inside job. Still, the handwriting provided no clue."

"Well, let's be thorough and give all of the staff a lie detector test," Frank said.

The Hardys told each employee about the surreptitious warning. No one seemed overly surprised to hear about it, although they all denied any knowledge of who sent it. Also, none of them objected to submitting to the polygraph test. In each case the results were negative.

Miss Hopkins, the nurse, said Mrs Retson was too ill to be questioned, and the boys did not pursue the matter. They repacked the equipment in thoughtful silence. They had drawn a blank. Besides being disappointed, they were slightly annoyed by the patronizing half-smile on Retson's face.

"Too bad," he said. "Now what kind of explanation can you come up with?"

"It'll take time to figure out," Frank said. "But there's an answer to everything. We'll solve this mystery sooner or later."

"I trust it will be sooner," Retson said as the Hardys left to return the polygraph. "I'm depending on your fine reputation as detectives to find my son!"

Frank and Joe were glum as they drove alongside a golf course on their way to Granite City Police Headquarters.

The green for the seventh hole lay close to the road, and a crawling sprinkler had come to rest near the edge of it, squirting water on to the pavement. Just as a car approached from the opposite direction, water splashed across the windshield of the Hardy's convertible, spraying them and momentarily blinding Frank's vision.

Cru-unch! They hit the oncoming car side on and came to a halt with screeching brakes.

Frank and Joe got out, as did two men from the other vehicle. One was a muscular individual wearing a slouch hat. His companion was young, slim, and had thick blond hair.

He managed a smile. "That was a pretty close shave," he said. "What happened? You seemed to swerve."

"Water from that sprinkler hit my windshield," Frank said.

The four circled the cars, examining the doors and bumpers. The convertible had a slight dent near the left door handle. The only damage to the other car was a scratch on the bumper.

The older man said, "If you're willing to overlook the dent, why don't you forget the small damage to my car? You know these insurance companies—miles of red tape."

"Fair enough," said Frank.

The man looked at the lie detector equipment in the back of the convertible and smiled. "Somebody's been put through a grilling, I see. You boys on the police force?"

"No, but we do detective work," Joe said.

"Are you on a case?"

"Yes, we're trying to pick up the trail of Graham Retson of Whisperwood."

"Ah, yes," the blond man said. "He disappeared some time ago. Think you can find him?"

"We hope to," Joe said.

"Come on," Frank urged. "We'd better be going. Thanks for your co-operation," he said, turning to the men. "Next time we'll be more careful about golf course sprinklers."

After the two cars had started off, Frank said, "Joe, you really yacked about our investigation. What's the idea?"

Joe looked embarrassed. "You're right, Frank. Sometimes I talk too much. I doubt, though, that those fellows had anything to do with the Retson mystery."

"Likely not, but there's no sense taking chances."

The boys returned the polygraph to the police. They thanked Chief Carton, who offered to co-operate with them in any way he could.

Then they drove back to Whisperwood. Frank parked the car near where the gardener was planting a small bush.

"This might be a good time to ask him a few questions," he said.

"Right," Joe agreed.

The boys walked up to the man. He was on his knees, firming the earth round the bush. When he saw the boys approaching, he looked up questioningly.

Frank came directly to the point. "Mr Jackson," he said, "how do you feel about young Graham's disappearance?"

The gardener trowelled some more earth on to the roots of the plant. "I just work here," he said calmly. "It's not my place to have any feelings about it."

"You must see a lot that goes on around here," Frank persisted. "Did Graham actually leave without you spotting him?"

"He did." Jackson was becoming surly. "I'm not his baby-sitter. And I don't keep a watch on the front door, either."

Just then the screen door of the kitchen opened. The gardener's wife stepped out. "I heard those questions about Graham Retson," she stated bluntly. "And let me tell you something. I'm glad that he's not cooped up here any more!"

"Can you help us find him, Mrs Jackson?" Joe asked.

"I wouldn't if I could," snapped the woman. "Why don't you mind your own business and leave the boy alone? He had good reason to run away!"

Mrs Jackson's tirade was interrupted by the sound of feet pounding along the brick walk. As Frank and Joe turned around, Chet Morton raced up to them.

His face was red from exertion. His breath came in big gulps. Wiping streams of perspiration from his forehead, he said, "Hey, fellows, I found out plenty!"

·4·

A Ghostly Figure

FRANK and Joe pulled Chet aside, and Frank asked, "What's up?"

"The Condor!" Chet puffed. "I've got the dope on it!"

"You mean the one that came through the window last night?"

"Not exactly," Chet answered. "But I've discovered who sells the Condor golf balls around here."

"Who's that?" Frank demanded.

"The golf pro at the Olympic Health Club. He's got a special concession. When you buy a Condor, you buy it from Gus McCormick."

"So Gus sold our ball to one of his customers?" Joe asked.

"That's my theory," Chet replied.

"That gives us something to go on," Joe said. "We'd better case the Olympic Health Club and see what gives over there."

Frank nodded. "That would be easy if Chet got a contract to retrieve golf balls from the Olympic water hazard."

Chet looked crestfallen. "Sorry, Frank. I've tried. I wangled two contracts from courses in town, but it was no dice at the Olympic. Say, I'd better get cracking with my suction pump. Business won't wait."

He left, and Frank and Joe resumed questioning the cook.

"Mrs Jackson," Frank said, "what did you mean when you said Graham had good reason to run away?"

"He wasn't happy here," she replied. "There were things he wanted to do that he wasn't allowed to."

"For instance?"

"Take those hamsters. They didn't do anyone any harm. And Graham got a lot of pleasure from them. Getting rid of them was a shame."

Her husband rose to his feet. "Be quiet, Martha!" he commanded. "You're talking too much."

"Mrs Jackson isn't revealing any secrets," Joe said.

"If Mr Retson wants to tell you about Graham, that's up to him," the gardener retorted. Turning to his wife, he asked crossly, "Do you want to get us fired?" He pulled her into the kitchen and the screen door slammed behind them.

Frank and Joe strolled over to the guesthouse.

"We've quizzed everybody except Mrs Retson," Frank pointed out. "She may have vital information about Graham. We'll have to talk to her."

"Retson might not go for the idea," Joe said. "Let's slip into the house when no one's looking."

As soon as darkness fell, the boys made their way through the grounds to the mansion. Circling round through the bushes, they reached the east wing of the building, prised open a window, and climbed over the sill into an unused room.

They went into the hallway and upstairs to the second floor where Mrs Retson had her apartment.

Joe knocked softly on the door. It opened. "What do you want?" asked Miss Hopkins.

"We'd like to speak to Mrs Retson," Frank said politely.

"Impossible! Mrs Retson doesn't receive visitors." The nurse started to shut the door, but Frank and Joe slipped past her before she realized what they were up to.

"Mrs Retson!" Frank called out, advancing towards the bedroom. "We must speak to you!"

"It's about Graham," Joe added. "And it's urgent."

The nurse followed, protesting all the while. No reply came from Mrs Retson. The three reached the bedroom doorway and peered in. They stood speechless.

The bed was empty!

Frank and Joe hastily searched the apartment. There was no sign of the woman anywhere. Joe pointed to an open window in the bedroom. A rope ladder was attached to the frame. "That's the explanation. She climbed out!"

"Your patient must be pretty agile," Frank said to the nurse as he looked out the window. Nobody was in sight.

"It's all your fault!" Miss Hopkins cried angrily. "When you barged in you must have frightened Mrs Retson. If anything happens to my patient I'll hold you responsible!" She pointed to the door. "Please leave immediately!"

"We're leaving," Frank assured her. "But we'll be back!"

As the boys went down the stairs, Frank said, "We'd better alert Retson that his wife is missing."

"Why don't we look for her first?" Joe suggested. "If

we tell him now, Hopkins might convince him it was
our fault."

"Okay. Let's make a quick search round the premises," Frank agreed.

The boys left the house by the same route they had
come in. They were about to split up when a loud cry
echoed through the night air. A single word rang in
their ears—a woman's voice screaming:

"Graham!"

Startled, Joe asked, "Where did that come from?"

"The waterfall. Come on!"

Frank pushed through the bushes and raced among
the trees with Joe at his heels. The roar of the falls
became louder with every step.

They turned up a narrow ravine. In the moonlight
they saw the water spilling over the edge of a rocky cliff.
It plunged into a churning whirlpool, from which a
stream with a strong current coursed along the side of
Granite Rock.

The Hardys moved towards the falls by stepping
gingerly from rock to rock, struggling to keep their
balance. "Once in that whirlpool," Frank warned,
"and it could be the last swim we ever take. Watch your
footing, Joe!"

The younger boy halted suddenly and pointed to the
top of the waterfall. "Look!" he yelled.

High above them on a boulder near the edge of the
drop stood the ghostly figure of a woman. Her head was
held high. Her body was tense. She stared into the
distance.

The boys wiped the spray from their eyes for a better
look, but a rising wind whipped a scarf across the
woman's face, concealing her features.

Frank was galvanized by the sight. "Joe, that woman may look like a wraith, but I'll bet she's Mrs Retson. I'm going to introduce myself."

The boys leaped over the rocky terrain. Suddenly Frank, who was behind Joe, lost his balance, clutched at the air, and fell into the water with a heavy splash.

The whirlpool took hold of Frank, bouncing him around like a cork. Desperately he struggled to escape from the swirling mass of water. A moment later he was thrown to one side. His head struck a rock with a thud and he blacked out.

Joe saw his brother go under, bob up, and float downstream. Frantically he dashed along the bank. Scrambling at breakneck speed across the boulders, he reached the spot where Frank was hurtling along helplessly towards certain death. Ahead was another drop full of razor-sharp rocks!

In the nick of time Joe reached down, grabbed Frank by the shirt collar, and dragged him to safety.

Frank lay quiet and Joe quickly applied mouth-to-mouth resuscitation until his brother regained consciousness. He gasped as he came round, "Thanks for fishing me out!"

Joe grinned. "As you said, this is no place for a swim."

Frank struggled to his feet. "The wraith—is she still up there?"

Both boys glanced towards the rock where the woman had been standing. A dense cloud covering the moon left the entire falls in darkness.

"She's probably gone by now," said Joe. "No use looking for her in this murk. We both might slip into the whirlpool next time."

"Joe, I didn't slip," Frank replied sombrely.

"What?"

"Somebody pushed me!"

"Did you see who it was?" Joe's voice was tense.

"No. But I think it was a man, judging by the force of the shove. He must have been lurking on the bank when I came along."

"Well, I didn't see anybody. I thought we were all alone at the bottom of the falls. Anyway, it proves something."

"Like what?" Frank asked.

"Somebody wants us off the Retson case. And he'll stop at nothing!"

"Which means we must be getting warm," Frank said. "Let's go back to the mansion. Perhaps Mrs Retson has returned by now."

They retraced their steps. As they approached the east wing, a figure way ahead of them ran across the lawn.

"A woman!" Frank exclaimed.

"Must be Mrs Retson!" Joe dashed off at top speed. Frank followed at a slower pace. But they were too late! The woman reached the building and began climbing up the side.

"She's going up the rope ladder!" Joe moaned.

"No doubt she's used to that contraption, the way she handles it," Frank said.

"Hey, what's this?" Joe said, picking up a piece of flimsy material torn from a scarf. He examined it for a moment, then put it in his pocket.

Since Frank was feeling exhausted from his ordeal in the whirlpool, they decided to call it a night. At the guesthouse Frank promptly fell into a deep sleep.

Joe lay in bed with his hands clasped behind his head, trying to make sense of the Retson riddle. "I wonder if Nurse Hopkins is in cahoots with Mrs Retson and knew where she went," he said to himself. Gradually he dozed off.

A hard pounding on the door snapped Joe wide awake. He looked at his watch. It was eight o'clock in the morning. Frank sat up, rubbing the sleep from his eyes. "What's all that noise about?" he asked groggily.

Joe got out of bed, opened the door, and confronted Harris the butler. He waved a cablegram wildly in Joe's face.

"It came this morning," he blurted out. "Now we know where Graham is!"

·5·

Away to Brazil

JOE seized the paper and read the message. *"Help,"* the cablegram said. *"Come Excelsior Grao Para. Do not reply. Just come. Graham."*

"You see," the butler remarked, "Graham must be in that hotel."

"Where is it?" asked Frank, who by now was wide awake.

"The cable was sent from Belem, Brazil. It's on the Amazon River, I believe."

"That's a strange place for him to be. Well, we'd better speak to Mr Retson right away."

"Yes, sir. He is waiting for you in his den," Harris said.

The Hardys found the tycoon looking very much relieved. "It's obvious what's happened," he chortled. "Graham has learned the error of his ways. He's got over all his nonsensical ideas and is ready to come home. The mystery is solved!"

"Looks as if there's nothing more for us to do," Joe observed.

"Wrong!" Retson retorted. "I hired you for an assignment, and it's still your case. Go to Brazil and escort my son home. Judging by his cablegram, he's in

41

some kind of trouble. Get him out of it, even if it's only an unpaid hotel bill."

Frank rubbed his chin thoughtfully. "That's okay by us, sir. But before we leave for Belem, we would like to talk with Mrs Retson."

The tycoon frowned. "Ordinarily I'd say no. But this new information about Graham is sure to cheer her up. Only make it short. I won't rest till I know you're on the plane to Brazil."

When Frank and Joe appeared at Mrs Retson's apartment, Miss Hopkins greeted them in stony silence. Had she told Retson about the incident the night before? Did she think the Hardys had? Her face showed nothing. She swung the door open and invited them in with a wave of her hand.

Mrs Retson was sitting in an armchair, a shawl over her shoulders and a blanket across her knees. Her head was tilted to one side and her eyes were half-closed. She seemed completely listless.

Frank suspected the woman was under sedation.

"Mrs Retson, we've come to ask you a few questions," Frank said.

The woman opened her eyes. "Questions? What kind of questions?"

"Well, we saw a woman at the waterfall last night. She resembled you!"

"It wasn't me!" Mrs Retson shuddered as she spoke and averted her eyes.

"This woman later climbed up a rope ladder to your room," Joe went on. "Who else could it have been?"

Mrs Retson's voice rose to a shrill pitch. "I don't know! I don't know! You must have made a mistake in the darkness."

"There was a full moon last night," Frank stated. "It lighted up the whole area of the waterfall."

"That explains what happened," she cried. "People often have delusions at the falls, especially under a full moon! You boys imagined you saw a woman."

Joe picked up a flimsy scarf from an easy chair. From his pocket he pulled the fragment of material he had found the previous night, and fitted it into a tear in the scarf. It matched perfectly.

Mrs Retson seemed terror-stricken at the sight. When Joe explained where the piece had come from, she slumped into unconsciousness.

"She's fainted!" Frank exclaimed. He began chafing her wrists while Joe massaged the back of her neck. Miss Hopkins came in quickly and held a glass of water to her lips.

Mrs Retson began to moan. She opened her eyes and gazed in bewilderment. After sipping a little water, she sat up. Joe adjusted the shawl, which had slipped down.

The nurse broke the silence. "That's enough. Mrs Retson isn't strong enough to be badgered like this. Do your investigating somewhere else!"

"We'll be leaving here soon," Joe promised. "We're going to Brazil to bring Graham home."

Upon hearing this, Mrs Retson raised a hand and cried out, "No! No! Graham is not in Brazil. He's right here!"

Startled, Frank begged her to explain herself. But she merely gave a knowing smile and refused to say another word.

Frank and Joe left the apartment, expecting the nurse to slam the door behind them. Instead, Miss

Hopkins joined the two of them in the hall.

"You must be mystified by Mrs Retson's remark," she said.

"That's putting it mildly," Joe replied.

Frank nodded in agreement. "What could she possibly have meant about Graham being right here?"

"She believes in extrasensory perception and psychic phenomena," Miss Hopkins explained. "She thinks a person can be in two places at once."

"So that's it," Frank said. "Thanks for telling us."

The boys went outside. Walking away from the mansion, they glanced back and looked up at Mrs Retson's apartment. They saw a face in the window. The woman herself was staring down at them with a pleading expression.

"I really feel sorry for her," Joe said. "She must be mentally ill. That explains her going down to the waterfall last night and calling Graham!"

The boys returned to the guesthouse. Chet Morton was there, and half an hour later Phil and Tony arrived. They had come to join Chet in the business of retrieving golf balls from the Granite City golf courses. The five discussed the latest events.

"So Joe and I will go to Brazil," Frank concluded. "Meanwhile, it would be a good idea if you guys could keep an eye on the Retson estate."

"How?" Chet asked. "You can't do it with a place this size from outside!"

"Maybe Retson will let you stay here. During part of the time you can scavenge golf balls, and when you're not busy, you can keep track of what's going on."

"Sounds good," Chet said with a grin. "It would save us money, too. Let's go see the big man."

The industrialist appeared gratified to know he could count on Chet, Phil, and Tony. "It'll be nice to have you fellows on the premises," he said. "Mrs Retson will feel much safer if we have muscular reinforcements as near as the guest-house. Not that I think anything will happen," he added.

Frank and Joe made plane reservations, then said goodbye to their pals and drove back to Bayport to get ready for the flight to Brazil. Their mother made lunch, then helped them pack their belongings. Laura Hardy always made sure the detectives in the family were properly equipped.

"I do hope you won't be gone long," she said.

"Not too long, Mom," Frank assured her. "It shouldn't take more than a few days."

"That's long enough to get caught by a boa constrictor or eaten by piranhas," came the voice of Aunt Gertrude, who had stepped into the boys' bedroom. "You'll probably get lost in the Amazon rain forest where the jaguars will take a bite out of you. Or the natives might nick you with their poison arrows."

"Aunt Gertrude, we're only going to Belem," Joe reminded her. "It's a modern city!"

"Anything can happen down there," Miss Hardy said sharply. "You boys had better look before you leap. Don't say I didn't warn you."

That evening Frank and Joe caught a connecting flight to New York. At Kennedy Airport they transferred to the jet to Brazil, and an hour later they were thundering through the air headed south.

The Hardys had the first two seats in their row. The window seat was occupied by a black-haired Brazilian in his early forties who spoke excellent English. He introduced himself in a friendly manner. "We will be on this plane for quite some time so we might as well get to know one another. My name is Joachim San Marten."

Frank introduced himself and his brother. "What kind of a city is Belem?" Joe asked their new acquaintance.

"Very romantic," San Marten replied. "It is at the mouth of the Amazon, and has buildings dating back to colonial times. Do not miss the Ver-O-Peso market. But remember that the Portuguese name means Watch-the-Weight. That's a wise rule to follow." He laughed.

Further conversation revealed that San Marten was a trader in wild animals.

"Zoos are always in the market for the snakes and big cats of the Amazon basin," he told the boys. "I buy them from the natives and ship them round the world. You have no doubt seen some of my animals in the United States. And why are you two gentlemen going to Belem?"

Frank said, "We're on our way to meet a friend in the city."

"Frank's afraid I'll spill the beans again," Joe thought and remained silent.

"Do you have good accommodations?"

"We are going to stay at the Excelsior Grao Para," Frank replied.

"Oh?" San Marten looked doubtful.

"What's the matter?"

"Nothing. It's just that this hotel has not the best reputation. It is said to be run by gangsters."

Frank grinned. "We'll watch out for the mob."

San Marten nodded. "Please remember, if I can be of any assistance, do not hesitate to call on me." He handed Frank his card.

"Thanks," Frank said. Then all three settled back in their seats for a snooze.

Hours later, in bright morning sunlight, the jetliner descended, and prepared for its landing at Belem. Through the window the boys could see the city. A riot of colour was reflected from red, green, and yellow tiled roofs. Small craft and freighters rocked gently in the harbour.

When they left the plane, the Hardys noticed San Marten waiting for a large crate that was being taken from the cargo compartment. It was covered by a tarpaulin.

"I wonder if one of our friend's dangerous animals is in there," said Joe.

"I suppose so," Frank replied. "Maybe he's brought back an American cougar for the Belem zoo."

After they were finished with the formalities at passport control and had claimed their baggage, they caught a taxi and soon arrived at the Excelsior Grao Para, which turned out to be a rather small hotel.

The desk clerk informed them that Mr Retson had checked out of his room.

"What? He's left?" Joe asked.

"Yes, sir. Mr Retson has departed."

"Where did he go?" Frank asked.

"He left no forwarding address."

"That's funny," Frank said, puzzled.

"Maybe he left a message for us in his room" Joe suggested. "Mind if we have a look?"

The clerk shrugged. "It's empty, so go ahead.

Number 225 he was in. I think it's open."

Frank and Joe left their bags at the desk, took the lift upstairs, and found the room. It was open and the key was in the lock. They walked inside.

"Let's give it a thorough once-over," Frank said.

They checked the dressers, the desk, and night table. Nothing. Frank searched the waste-paper basket but found no clues. Joe opened the closet. "Hey, here's something!" he said.

Joe brought out a leather jacket. It bore a label from a Granite City store. Methodically he searched the pockets. In one of them was a cigarette lighter.

"Look at his," Joe said. Out of curiosity he flipped the top open.

A sharp needle sprang out from a hidden trap.

It pierced Joe's thumb. He staggered back with a cry, went rigid for a split second, and then toppled over, unconscious!

·6·

Underground Voodoo

FRANK rushed over to where his brother lay on the floor. "Joe, what happened?"

Joe made no reply. His eyes were closed, and his face was pale. He breathed heavily as if gasping for air.

"I've got to get a doctor fast," Frank thought desperately. He went to the door, twisted the old-fashioned knob, and jerked hard. It did not budge! He tried shouting for help, but nobody heard him.

Frank ran to the telephone beside the bed. The desk failed to answer. Frantically, Frank poked his head out the window. There was a fire escape, but his heart sank when he saw that the bottom part of the ladder had been removed, leaving a thirty-foot drop to the pavement. He would need a rope!

Frank pulled the sheets from the bed, tore them into strips, and knotted the pieces together. Then he started to climb out the window.

Suddenly a click at the door caused him to turn round. "Hello?"

The door opened and San Marten stepped in. He looked in amazement at the torn sheets in Frank's hands and at Joe lying unconscious on the floor.

"What's going on here?" he asked.

"Quick, I need a doctor for Joe," Frank said. "He's been poisoned."

San Marten ran to the phone. The desk answered and he called for the hotel physician.

While they waited, Frank asked, "How did you get in here, and why did you come?"

"The key was on the other side and the door unlocked," San Marten replied. "I was in the neighbourhood and decided you might need some help in a strange city. The clerk told me you were up here. How was your brother poisoned?"

Just then the doctor hastened in. He set down his bag and kneeled beside Joe. After feeling the boy's pulse, he asked, "What caused it?"

Frank indicated the lighter. The doctor examined it closely. Then he pulled a syringe out of his bag and gave Joe an injection.

"The young man will be all right," he said. "But he could not have lasted much longer. He is suffering from a powerful poison. Fortunately he has a strong heart or he would be dead by now!"

"This seems to be a fiendish plot!" San Marten declared. "You will have to take precautions."

"Somebody in Belem doesn't like us," Frank agreed. "I'm glad you do, Mr San Marten. It's nice to have a friend in a strange city."

"I am happy to have been of assistance," San Marten replied. "If you take my advice, you will not remain at this hotel. Go somewhere else."

"We will," Frank assured him, "as soon as Joe's back on his feet."

While they were speaking, Joe came round. The doctor examined him and said he was out of danger.

When Joe stood up, he wobbled. "I'm a trifle queasy," he said. But gradually he felt stronger and the physician left.

"Incidentally," San Marten said, "where is the friend you were looking for?"

"We don't know. He checked out before we arrived," Frank replied.

"It is strange that the young man departed so suddenly," San Marten said. "Perhaps something happened to him."

"Graham must have been in a tizzy," Joe agreed. "After all, he left without his jacket."

"And his cigarette lighter," Frank added. "That is, if it was really his."

A bellboy opened the door and San Marten called him in.

"Perhaps you can give us some information about the former occupant of this room?"

"Yes, sir. A very rich American by the name of Graham Retson. About my age."

"What became of him?" Frank asked eagerly. "Did he say anything to you about where he was going?"

"All I can tell you is that he left the hotel in the company of two men. I do not know what their destination was."

"Did you know the men?" Joe asked.

"One of them," the bellboy stated. "I have seen him before many times at the Ver-O-Peso market. But I do not know his name or what he does."

Close questioning of the bellboy elicited no further information and he left.

"If you like, I will be glad to take you to the Ver-O-Peso market to look for your friend," San Marten said.

"We'd appreciate it," Frank said.

The boys took a room at the hotel, then sallied out into Belem with the Brazilian.

Crowds of people streamed past them on the streets. Rickety cars bumped over the cobblestones. A wisp of smoke drifting by carried the scent of roasting nuts.

San Marten smiled as he sniffed the aroma. "Nuts are one of the most important exports of our country. See this truck? Those big bags piled on top are full of Brazil nuts."

Joe noticed a monkey climb to the top of the sacks. He was about to call attention to him when suddenly one of the bags moved.

"Frank! Jump!" Joe yelled.

The massive bag smashed on the cobblestones where Frank had been. The truck stopped, the monkey disappeared, and the driver recovered his cargo.

"Thanks for the warning, Joe," Frank said. "I'd hate to be knocked off the case by a bag of nuts. But accidents will happen."

Joe was not convinced that it was an accident. The monkey had pushed the nuts. Could someone have put him up to it? Or was he just monkeying around?

The three stopped for lunch in a small restaurant, then continued on to the colourful market. They walked between stalls heaped with tropical fruits, sandals, and gewgaws.

Sellers offered their wares, buyers scoffed at prices, and haggling went on amid a din of Portuguese epithets.

Joe gestured towards one of the stalls. "How about a baby python, Frank? Or maybe you'd settle for some alligator teeth?"

"No thanks. I think I'll take a voodoo charm home to Aunt Gertrude," Frank replied.

Joe tried to find an opportunity to tell his brother about the monkey but San Marten did not leave their side.

Finally they stopped in front of a witchcraft stall, where a wizened, gnome-like old man offered to sell them weird idols, magical potions, and wax figures in which to stick pins.

San Marten spoke to the man in Portuguese, and turned to the boys. "We're invited to join a voodoo rite. Buru here claims he can conjure up a vision of where your friend is."

The witch doctor smiled and nodded, showing broken teeth.

"Tell him we don't believe in visions," Frank said.

San Marten smiled. "I'm sure you don't. But these dances are interesting to watch, and you do not get a chance like this often."

Frank shrugged. "Okay."

San Marten again spoke in Portuguese to the witch doctor, who bowed and gestured. Then he led the way through his stall, between piles of dried snake skins and jungle herbs, to a small door at the rear. He opened it, and a narrow spiral stone staircase lay before them.

Cackling softly to himself, Buru lifted a battered lantern off the wall, lighted it, and descended. The air became cool and the stone walls dripped moisture. The lantern threw flickering rays of light that only made the darkness behind seem more intense.

The old man stopped in front of a heavy wooden door and spoke in his native tongue. San Marten translated: "We are in an underground cellar far below the level of the street. The magical rites are held down here to prevent unwelcome intrusions by unbelievers, especially the police!"

The police! A shiver ran down Frank's spine. What kind of a place were they being taken to?

Buru pulled out a black key. The lock clicked and the door opened into a large musty room. Enormous dust-coated beams supported the high ceiling.

About twenty silent natives sat in a circle on the stone floor. All were dressed in flowing white robes. An earthenware jug passed from hand to hand around the circle, each man taking a swig as it reached him.

"My friends," San Marten whispered, "you have entered the world of macumba."

"Macumba?" Joe asked, puzzled. "What's that?"

"A form of voodoo. These people are convinced they can bring back departed spirits by means of a magical dance. The spirit possesses one of the dancers."

"They're not dancing now," Frank remarked.

"They are preparing for it by drinking the secret brew. A vile concoction, I assure you. I tasted it once."

The macumba mediums began swaying from side to side. They broke into a rhythmical chant and clapped their hands.

"This is the sacred song," San Marten explained. "By chanting these verses, they seek to placate the dead and open the path of communication."

The shadowy faces assumed ecstatic expressions as the Hardys watched. In the lamplight black eyes glowed like embers. The chant rose to a soaring crescendo.

Suddenly the nearest man got to his feet and began a jig. One by one the others imitated him, until they were all on their feet, stamping and waving their hands.

The circle began to move. Fascinated, Frank drew closer. The wild-eyed macumba dancers seemed to have hypnotized him. As if drawn by an invisible magnet, he moved into the middle of the ring, which revolved faster and faster.

Suddenly a piercing shriek brought Frank out of his trance. One of the natives fell to the floor, clutching at his throat. The others screamed and danced more wildly.

Frank looked around. The hair rose on the back of his neck.

"This is ridiculous," he thought. "I have to get out of here." He plunged between two of the dancers, looking for his brother and San Marten. A chill went down his spine when he realized that they were no longer with him.

Frank began a systematic search, making his way to the rear of the circle, and walking once around. No luck! Again he pressed himself between the ecstatically gyrating bodies to the centre. San Marten and Joe were nowhere in sight! Had they left?

Frank looked for the door. It had disappeared, too! His pulse beat like a jackhammer. He was trapped amid the zealots of voodoo!

·7·

Buru's Vision

WITH sinuous movements, hands reached out towards Frank. Was he about to become a victim of macumba rites?

"Not if I can help it," he thought. "I'll go down swinging before I let those lunatics get me!" He assumed a judo stance, ready to hit the first attacker with a karate chop.

"Cool it, Frank," came a low familiar voice. "It's me."

"Joe?" Frank was dumbfounded. In the dim light he could barely make out his brother's features.

"Right. Don't let the party costume fool you. I just put it on for this shindig. Same for my dancing partner here. He's not what he seems."

Frank recognized San Marten. "What's the big idea?" he demanded.

"San Marten suggested joining the dance," Joe said. "I figured you were coming, too."

"I thought we might learn something that would lead us to Graham Retson," San Marten said.

"Down here with these weirdos?" Frank shook his head. "Let's get out of here. We can resume our conference when we get away from these shimmy-shakers."

The voodoo dancers were becoming more frenzied. Their chanting became stentorian, and their contortions more furious.

Frank saw Buru coming towards them as Joe and San Marten slipped back into their own clothes. The old man motioned to them, then led the way around the dancing circle, edging along so as not to attract attention, to a point where a big stone block stood against the wall.

Gesturing to the others to help, he began to push at the block. The rest pitched in, shifted the obstruction to one side, and gained access to an opening through which they had to crawl on their hands and knees.

They reached another stone staircase. Hastening upwards, they returned to the witch doctor's stall. With their hands they shielded their eyes from the daylight until they became reaccustomed to it.

The two Brazilians began an animated conversation. Frank tugged at Joe's sleeve and the boys moved off to one side, out of earshot.

"Wow! Am I glad to be back on earth!" Frank said.

Joe grinned. "Actually, it was fun!" Then he became serious. "A lot of strange things have happened since our arrival," he said. "That bag of nuts which fell off the truck, for instance. It was pushed by a monkey!"

"That figures," Frank said. "Somebody's after us. And I'd include San Marten among the suspects. I haven't yet discovered why he's so concerned about us."

"I think he's okay," Joe said.

"Maybe so. But I don't see why he brought us to this place. He can't take that voodoo stuff seriously."

"Of course not. He just thought it would be interesting for us to watch. I guess it was, too!"

"And what about his showing up at the hotel just at the right time? He claimed the door was open, but I'll bet somebody locked it after we went into the room. And how come part of the fire escape ladder was missing just when I needed it?"

"How's that again?"

Frank told his brother about his movements while Joe had been unconscious. "When I tried to call for a doctor, I got no answer. After San Marten had come in, the desk answered immediately."

"That doesn't prove anything. The clerk might have had another call."

"And how do you explain the locked door?"

"It could have been stuck."

"Then the bellboy walked in when nobody called for him."

"He might have been sent to take out the dishes. I saw a tray and a couple of glasses on one of the dressers."

Frank sighed. "Maybe you're right, but the whole thing is too pat, too—"

Just then San Marten beckoned to the Hardys. "Buru has a prediction about where to find Graham. He says he had a vision that your friend is going up the Amazon to Manaus."

"Where's that?"

"It's a port near the juncture of the Amazon and the Negro rivers nearly a thousand miles from here."

"Baloney!" Frank murmured to Joe.

The witch doctor sensed their scepticism. He smiled and spoke volubly.

San Marten said, "He warns that we had better

believe his vision. Otherwise serious harm might come to Graham. If you want to find him, go to Manaus."

"We'll think it over," Frank began, "and when we reach—"

He was interrupted by a rustling sound at the back of the stall. Furry fingers pulled the curtains apart. A simian face appeared in the opening. Frank and Joe saw a howler monkey about three feet tall, with silky black fur and a savage expression.

The Hardys got only a brief glimpse before the face pulled back behind the curtains.

"So you keep a monkey for a pet, Buru," Joe said.

When San Marten translated that remark, the witch doctor shook his head angrily and went into a torrent of negatives.

"He denies he has a monkey on the premises," San Marten reported.

"We saw it!" Frank insisted.

"Buru says that whatever you saw was caused by your imagination."

"Like his visions," Joe scoffed.

San Marten smiled. "Perhaps. Still I believe it would be better if I left your comparison untranslated. Witch doctors are not the best-tempered people in Belem."

Joe looked amused. "You mean Buru might place a curse on us?"

Sensing hostility, Frank said, "We'd better return to the Excelsior Grao Para."

"Not there, my friends," San Marten protested. "My home in the suburbs is at your disposal. Please use it freely as long as you stay in Belem."

Frank and Joe, however, would not be swayed. "You see," Frank stated, "we need to be in the city while looking for our friend. Thanks all the same."

"Some other time," Joe promised. "We'll take a rain-check just now."

They parted with friendly handshakes, and the boys went to the hotel. The desk clerk waved to them. "Mr Retson returned while you were out."

"Is he here now?" Joe asked excitedly.

"No. He came for his leather jacket and departed again."

"Did he give you any forwarding address this time?" Frank queried.

"All he said was that he was going to Manaus, and that he could not wait. He mentioned no address in that city."

The boys went to their room and Joe closed the door. "Good heavens, Frank! Buru was right. It's incredible!"

Frank suspected trickery. Joe, on the other hand, felt that the voodoo witch doctor might have some psychic power of insight. They discussed the case from every angle and tried to figure out how to proceed from here.

"Now we're faced with the monkey mystery, too!" Frank said. "Are you sure that sack of nuts was pushed by the monkey?"

"Listen, Frank. I told you!"

"Okay, okay. Don't let this give us the jitters. Was it the same one we saw at Buru's?"

"I don't know," Joe said. "Monkeys all look alike to me."

Frank sagged into a chair and let out a long breath. "San Marten bugs me."

"You worry too much," Joe said. "Tell you what. If it will make you feel better, why not have Dad inquire about him at the Brazilian Embassy in Washington?"

"Good thinking. We'll send Dad a cable."

"What about Manaus?"

"It's our only clue. I suggest we go, but proceed with extreme caution."

"I'm with you," Joe said. He took out a cablegram blank from the desk drawer and wrote: *Need info Brazil Embassy Joachim San Marten. On way to Manaus re Graham.*

"I'll take it down to the telegraph office," he said when he was finished. "Better not trust the bellboy with it."

"I'll go with you," Frank said. "I'm starved."

The boys had dinner in a small restaurant near the hotel, then returned to their room. It was not air conditioned and seemed like an oven.

"We'd better get as much air as we can," Frank suggested, forcing the window wide open.

"Come to think of it," Joe said, "the fire escape would be a good place to sleep on a night like this. Natural air conditioning."

They showered and then turned in. Frank placed a flashlight on the table beside the bed for emergency use, which was an old habit with him.

Both boys slept fitfully, turning and tossing on sweat-dampened sheets. Suddenly both were wide awake. There was a strange noise in their room. Dimly they made out a figure bending over their clothes.

"A thief!" Joe thought.

Carefully Frank reached for his flashlight. Pointing it towards the intruder, he snapped it on. A cone of light stabbed through the darkness. It revealed a hideous-looking simian standing beside a chair, holding Frank's shirt in one of its paws. The monkey's nose was wrinkled, the eyes drawn into narrow glaring slits, and his fangs were bared in a ferocious scowl!

·8·
Fish Bait

FRANK and Joe jumped up and dived for the simian. Joe got a hand on a furry leg, but the animal scampered free. It dashed to the fire escape and swung down the metal framework from floor to floor, using its long prehensile tail as a fifth paw. The boys watched in dismay as the monkey finally leaped to the pavement and vanished around a corner of the hotel.

"That's the ugliest brute I've ever seen," Joe said in a shaky voice. "I'd consider it a nightmare if you hadn't seen it too, Frank."

"Oh, it was real enough," said Frank, who had been examining his clothes. "Real enough to make off with my wallet, key ring, passport and other identification papers."

Joe went through his pockets. "Good grief! I'm cleaned out, too!"

Frank sat down on the bed. "Joe, we're dealing with a monkey clever enough to be a professional burglar. A human being couldn't have pulled off the job more neatly."

"A human being put that monkey up to it!" Joe said.

An odd feeling swept over both boys. They felt as if they were in the grip of some evil power, as if a malevolent force was bent on their destruction.

"Frank," Joe said, "we're stuck. No money, no passports, no nothing. What'll we do?"

"Go to the American Consulate," Frank said. "Then I suggest we call San Marten and tell him our sad story. If he's involved in it, we might as well stick close to him. He doesn't know we suspect him, so maybe we can pick up a clue."

At nine in the morning Frank asked the hotel clerk to put him through to San Marten's home. After a brief wait, the Brazilian's voice came over the wire. Frank told him they had been robbed.

"I will help you," San Marten assured them. "Come here for breakfast. Take a taxi at my expense. I will instruct my servants to set two extra places."

Frank and Joe accepted his invitation, but first made their way to the consulate. A United States official gave them some cash, arranged for them to cable home for money, and promised to have identification for them shortly.

The boys thanked him, caught a taxi in front of the consulate, and reached the suburbs of Belem in about twenty minutes. It was an exclusive residential area of large houses with broad lawns. Maids were sweeping off front porches and washing windows. Gardeners were spading the earth.

"Nice area," Joe commented. "The rich live well here, too."

The Brazilian's home turned out to be a plush one. A wrought-iron gate gave access to a walk flanked by tropical flowers leading up to a big house. The door was opened by a servant who ushered the boys through to a patio in the rear of the property.

San Marten sat at a table beside a broad, deep swimming pool. Thick shrubbery grew a few yards from the pool on three sides; the fourth side facing the house was open.

San Marten rose. "I am very happy to see you here," he said, waving them to a couple of empty chairs.

Frank noticed the table was placed on the west side of the pool in the morning sun. They sat down with their backs to the glare.

A second servant brought in a platter of ham and eggs, which the boys ate with great relish. At the same time they discussed the theft by the monkey. San Marten seemed thoroughly mystified. He folded his napkin and placed it on the table.

"I will speak to the police immediately," he said.

"We'll go with you," Frank said.

"That won't be necessary. You stay here and relax. Enjoy a swim in the pool," San Marten said. "You'll find suits in the cabana."

Before they could object, he stepped into a light-blue sports car parked nearby and roared off in the direction of Belem.

Frank and Joe sat lazily in the sun for a while, then Joe said, "I think I'll take San Marten up on his swim invitation. How about you?"

"First we'll get rid of the breakfast dishes," Frank said with a grin. "Aunt Gertrude would never approve if we left the table like this."

He rang the bell for the servants, expecting someone to come and clean up the table. Receiving no response, he went into the house, found it empty, and returned to the patio.

"The help has vamoosed as well," he told Joe.

"Must be their day off," his brother guessed. "We'll have some peace and quiet for our dip."

"They were here when we arrived, so it's hardly their day off," Frank said, an uneasy feeling coming over him. "I think maybe San Marten is up to something."

Joe had already started for the cabana and quickly slipped into a pair of trunks which looked as if they would fit. Frank followed suit, still pondering the strange disappearance of the servants. As they emerged from the cabana, the sunlight reflected from the surface of the pool in blinding rays. Joe climbed on the diving board, where he poised for a back somersault.

Frank, shielding his eyes, spotted a slight movement down in the water. Suddenly Aunt Gertrude's warning rang in his ears: "Look before you leap!"

Leaning over the edge of the pool, he saw a small fish not more than eight inches long. It had a blunt face with an underslung jaw, a silvery bluish body, and a touch of red on its fins.

"Joe, don't dive!" Frank shouted.

The warning came almost too late and Joe had trouble regaining his balance. "Why, what's the matter?" he asked.

"You'll have company you may not care to meet. Come here!"

Joe descended from the diving board and peered down at the fish.

"Frank, there's more than one. In fact, a whole school. Wait a minute! I have a hunch!" Joe ran to the table where the breakfast dishes still lay. Seizing a piece of ham from the platter, he returned to the pool.

He tossed the ham through the air. It hit the water with a splash and had hardly started to sink when the school of small fish darted to it. They became a swirling horde of ferocious predators, tearing off mouthfuls and gulping them down. The ham was gone in seconds!

Frank and Joe shuddered.

Piranhas!

"No wonder San Marten and the servants vanished so suddenly," Frank muttered. "They set up operation bone yard for our benefit, but didn't want to witness the gory details. And the table was set up facing the sun to keep us from spotting the fish."

"Wow! I'm beginning to feel sick," Joe said.

"Come on," Frank said. "I've got an idea." He led the way into the kitchen and opened the refrigerator. They found a rib roast, two large hams, a big loin of pork and a leg of lamb.

"Our host must have been planning a party," Frank said. "Joe, help me carry these!"

The boys lugged the meat outside. "In they go!" Frank said as they tossed the provisions into the water.

The piranhas were on them in a flash. The water boiled with the assault. In a few minutes only cleaned bones lay at the bottom of the pool.

Suddenly the front door slammed. Frank and Joe dodged into the shrubbery, crouched down, and parted the leaves. The two servants walked warily across the patio to the pool.

One laughed, elbowed his companion, and pointed to the bones. The other guffawed as if he had just heard a good joke.

"They think they're looking at our remains," Joe whispered.

Frank nodded. "We'd better get off the premises before they find out the truth. Come on!"

As they slipped through the shrubbery Joe tripped and fell. Frank paused to help him up. Then came the sound of pursuers.

The boys careered past large bushes and small trees towards the fence at the back of the property. Frank scrambled to the top. Joe followed, barely escaping the clutching fingers of one of the servants.

"They'll come after us!" Joe panted.

They ran down the street and turned a corner.

"In there!" Frank replied, pointing to the nearest building. It was a low neat structure with the sign BIBLIOTECA beside the front door.

"It's a library," Frank said. "And look how we're dressed."

The dark-haired, pretty girl at the reception desk was startled by the sudden appearance of two boys in swimming trunks. Readers looked up from their books and newspapers to see what all the commotion was about.

The boys asked for help and the girl, in halting English, said, "I will get police. You wait."

Frank and Joe squatted behind some bookshelves. A few minutes later a squad car transported the Hardys to headquarters. The chief, Captain Vasquez, spoke English quite well.

Frank asked for San Marten, but was told he had not come to headquarters. Then the boys went over the morning's events repeatedly, only to be met with grins of disbelief.

"Americanos good with joke!" said a lieutenant, bursting into loud laughter.

"Joachim San Marten would never do anything like this," the captain insisted. "He is a respectable man."

"Send your men to investigate his swimming pool," Frank urged.

Vasquez hummed and hawed, but finally agreed. The squad car went out. It returned ten minutes later and the two policemen reported nothing unusual about San Marten's pool.

Frank was crushed. "The servants must have removed the piranhas and the bones," he said weakly.

"We will forget your fish story," Vasquez said, shaking his head, "and let you go this time. Get out of these swimming trunks. We will find your size among clothing left by former prisoners."

"Thanks," Joe said glumly, disappointed that nobody believed them.

The boys changed, then left. As they walked into the lobby of the Excelsior Grao Para, Frank grabbed his brother's elbow. "Sh! Look over there at the desk!"

"San Marten!" Joe gasped.

The Brazilian was in a towering fury. His face was flushed, his body trembling. He pounded the desk with his fist.

"Where are the Hardys?" San Marten demanded in English.

"Sir, I have no idea."

San Marten seized the man by the lapels and shook him. "Where did they go? Where can I find them?"

"Sir, if I knew, believe me I would tell you," the clerk gasped.

Thrusting him aside with a contemptuous gesture, San Marten wheeled round. The Hardys hastily ducked behind a large pillar. Had they been fast enough? Had their murderous enemy seen them?

·9·

A Curious Number Seven

SAN MARTEN motioned savagely in the Hardys' direction. He started walking towards the pillar behind which they were hiding.

"He's spotted us!" Joe warned.

"Get ready," Frank muttered. "We'll have to fight our way out of this one!"

San Marten's vigorous strides brought him quickly abreast of the pillar. The boys could see the angry tightening of his jaw. Tensely they prepared for a counter-attack.

The Brazilian, however, did not circle the pillar. He walked straight past towards a man in the doorway at whom he had been gesturing. The pair disappeared out of the hotel.

Frank mopped the perspiration from his forehead. "Wow! That was close."

"Let's scram while we're still in one piece," Joe urged.

"Right. But we'll need our suitcases."

"How do we get to the room—by asking the clerk for the key?"

Frank grinned. "I'd rather not. Let's take the fire escape. Since we paid one night in advance when we registered, I suggest we forget about checking out, too."

The boys managed to climb up to their window unseen. They jumped into the room, took their bags, and went out the same way.

"Where to now?" Joe asked.

"There's a park a few blocks down the street," Frank said. "San Marten won't think of looking for us there. We'll have to hang around for a while until money from home arrives."

They found the park practically deserted. Seated on a bench under some spreading tropical foliage, they were able to talk freely with no fear of eavesdroppers.

"San Marten can't be operating against us all on his lonesome," Joe remarked. "He must be the leader of a gang."

Frank agreed. "Try this for size, Joe. The gang kidnapped Graham Retson, took the money he withdrew from the bank, and are now holding him for ransom. They're out to get us before we rescue Graham."

"You're on my wavelength, Frank, coming through loud and clear."

Frank paused to think over the problem. "I can't figure out where Manaus fits in. That clue might be a plant to lure us up the Amazon so San Marten and company can ambush us."

"On the other hand," Joe countered. "Graham could really be in Manaus. Our job is to find him, so we can't ignore the whole thing."

"Besides," Frank said, "if it's a trap, we may be able to turn the tables on the gang. Forewarned is forearmed, as Aunt Gertrude would say."

"I'll buy that," Joe said. "But how do we get to

Manaus? If we take a boat upriver, it'll take weeks before we arrive."

"We'll have to fly."

"San Marten will have the commercial lines watched," Joe predicted. "And I doubt if we can rent a plane without identification papers. That second-storey monkey grounded us."

"Maybe the man at the consulate can give us some advice," Frank said. "We'll have to check in there anyhow for our money. I hope it has arrived."

Carrying their bags, Frank and Joe returned to the American Consulate, which was near the park. The man they had spoken to that morning greeted them with a smile. "Your money is here," he said. "I'm having your passports cancelled and you will have new ones soon."

Frank explained that they wanted to fly to Manaus and the man made a quick phone call. He spoke in Portuguese, smiled, and hung up.

"This should do the trick," he said to the Hardys. "Go to the airport on the edge of town. A pilot by the name of Rico Armand is waiting there. He has a small private plane and will fly you to Manaus."

"Thank you very much," Frank said, and the Hardys walked out of the office.

They hailed a taxi and an hour later were at the airport. They found the pilot, a handsome youth in his early twenties, who spoke English.

Armand shook hands, mentioned his fee, and the boys paid in advance. Then the three took off.

They circled over the vast delta of the Amazon, heading upriver. The east coast disappeared behind them, and the rain forest extended on both sides like a huge green carpet. It looked never-ending.

Smaller tributary streams could be seen snaking through towering trees before emptying into the broad river.

The plane flew on and on, and it seemed nothing else existed in the world exept those countless miles of jungle beneath their wings.

Two refuelling stops were made at intermediate air-strips. Armand followed the Rio Negro from its confluence with the Amazon, and finally Manaus came into sight.

Frank and Joe looked down on hundreds of canoes in the river, paddled by natives headed for the waterfront market with cargoes of fruit and vegetables. The build-ings of the city were a conglomeration of styles, running from primitive huts to old colonial and modern high-rise buildings.

One building in particular stood out—an ornate structure of pink and white marble. Frank and Joe stared in disbelief.

"How did that ever get into the jungle?" Joe asked.

"That's the old opera house," Armand replied. "Manaus used to be the rubber capital of Brazil. The wealthy planters had the best of everything, including opera."

"The city must have gone downhill since then," Frank remarked.

"Brazil's rubber doesn't sell too well these days," said the pilot. "Can't compete with the East Indies. So Manaus is pretty much what you Americans would call a ghost town of the Amazon."

"How do people make a living now?" Joe asked.

"Partly from tourism. Manaus is a free port and you

can buy things duty free. That's one reason I see more visitors in Manaus every time I come."

A message from the airport tower came over the radio: "Wait for permission to land." Armand began to circle. His fuel gauge showed the plane could not keep flying much longer.

"I don't understand the delay," he said nervously. "I'll have to land without permission if this keeps up."

"Frank," Joe muttered, "this may be San Marten's doing."

The fuel gauge pointed to *empty* and the three aboard were braced for a crash landing when the control tower finally gave the okay.

"Down to the last drop of fuel," Armand commented as they taxied to a halt. In the terminal they found out that a maintenance truck had been stalled on the runway.

After a quick sandwich at the airport the boys said goodbye to the pilot, then took a taxi to a hotel in the middle of town. After checking in they began to scout Manaus for Graham Retson. None of the hotels had any record of him, so they turned their attention to the rooming houses. It was not until the next day, however, that they struck a lead.

"Yes," said the owner of a small rooming house, a German named Bauer, "Graham Retson was here, but left yesterday. I found this paper in his room. Maybe it will help you."

Frank took the piece of paper. It was dirty and wrinkled as if it had been crumpled into a ball and tossed aside. He examined the crudely scrawled message. It was dated May seventh and said: "I am being taken to a small boat next to the Argentine freighter in

Manaus harbour. My captors intend to take me farther up the Amazon. Help! Graham Retson.''

Joe whistled and pulled his brother aside. "Frank, this is a real clue!"

"You're wrong, Joe."

"Why?"

"Look at the date. The seven has a bar through it. That's the European way of writing the number. No American would do it like that. Another thing. Today is May seventh. The landlord said Graham left yesterday. He's in cahoots with San Marten, Joe! Bauer wrote the note himself. They're trying to trick us!"

"We'll trick them in return!" Joe declared. "They want to get us aboard their boat for a one-way voyage to the bottom of the Amazon. Instead, we'll stay off the boat and listen to what's going on."

"With our bug, you mean?" Frank asked. "Great idea."

The boys went back to their hotel. Frank opened his suitcase and drew out a length of coiled wire from a hidden pocket under a false bottom. One end of the wire had a set of earphones attached. From the other dangled a sensitive metal sphere. The Hardys had often used this detection device to listen in on conversations at long range.

They walked to the harbour at nightfall. Frank pointed to the lights of a hulking vessel anchored there. "That's the Argentine freighter, Joe. And that small boat beside it has to be the one we're looking for."

"Okay, I'll go to work."

Frank, holding the earphones, sat down behind some crates on the dock. Joe stripped quickly to his shorts, then slipped into the river carrying the wire, which payed out from the bank as he swam. Reaching the boat, he carefully planted the bug on one of the port-holes.

"The insect is ready to strike," Joe announced when he came back to Frank, shaking the droplets of water off his body. Then he began to put on his slacks and shirt.

"Hurry," Frank said suddenly. "We're having company."

Two men walked down to the water's edge and stopped a few yards from where the Hardys were concealed. Obviously convinced that they were alone in the darkness, they spoke clearly in English. The Hardys recognized the voices.

"San Marten!" Joe whispered.

Frank nodded. "The other guy sounds like Bauer—that guy at the rooming house."

San Marten spoke in more informal English than they had ever heard him use before. "Are you positive every angle's covered? I don't want any slips, mind you."

"Don't get upset," his companion replied. "Diabo is standing guard. No one can sneak past him. He's foolproof."

"Okay," San Marten said with satisfaction. "Soon the river will have the Hardys."

"Joachim, that was a good idea to lure them to Brazil. With Graham on our hands back north at—"

A sudden noise caused Frank and Joe to whirl round.

They saw the monkey with the evil face charging at them! He was so close that they did not have a chance to move. Snapping and snarling ferociously the animal catapulted into the Hardys. The force of the assault toppled them over into the river!

·10·

Adrift on the Amazon

FRANK and Joe plummeted down through the water until they steadied themselves. Kicking convulsively, they shot back to the surface.

At once the howler monkey was on them, clawing their backs with his hind paws, nipping and scratching at their heads.

Frank twisted around and pulled the creature off Joe. Their combined strength was too much even for their savage assailant. Suddenly the monkey wrenched himself from their grasp. Streaking through the water, he made for the shore.

"Don't let him get away!" Frank spluttered.

But a fusillade of shots changed the Hardys' minds. Bullets skipped off the surface of the river and whined into the darkness.

Joe halted abruptly, treading water. He turned back towards Frank. "We can't get to the shore," he warned.

"Let's swim downstream," Frank suggested.

"And quick," Joe said. "They're coming after us!"

The *put-put* of a motorboat echoed across the water, growing louder as the craft cut the distance between it and the boys. Frantically Frank and Joe swam out into the river. The motorboat gained on them rapidly.

Just then a pleasure launch came gliding in their direction. The lights of the cabin threw a sheen over the Rio Negro. Three or four couples were dancing to the rhythm of a small band.

"Follow me!" Frank gasped. "To the other side!"

Waiting until the launch was slightly upstream from him, he took a deep breath and submerged. Kicking hard, and using his arms in a powerful breaststroke, he arched down under the launch. The keel scraped his back as he passed. His lungs were bursting for want of air when he came up on the opposite side of the craft. Reaching out, he grasped a railing just above the water line.

A split second later Joe bobbed up beside him. They clung to the railing side by side, gasping for breath. The launch carried them swiftly down the river.

"Now what?" Joe asked. "Shall we call the skipper?"

"Better not," Frank said. "There's no telling who's on board. San Marten's confederates would be only too happy to arrange a reception committee for us."

They clung to the launch until it passed the confluence of the Rio Negro and the Amazon, a few miles below Manaus. Feeling safe, they dropped off and swam to the shore.

"I've had it," Frank said, flopping down in a patch of tall jungle grass.

"Rest a while," Joe said. "I'll get us a snack."

He walked off into the jungle and returned ten minutes later with a big bunch of bananas. Voraciously they ate the fruit, tossing the skins over their shoulders as they worked through the bunch.

"At least we won't starve here," Frank observed.

"We're okay," Joe said, "as long as we don't get

eaten. I'd hate to wake up and find a hungry jaguar staring me in the eye."

"There's probably a lot of them in this area," Frank said. "Hear those monkeys chattering in the trees? Jaguars feast on monkeys."

Joe pondered Frank's remark. "That reminds me. We've learned the name of the beast that's been annoying us—Diabo."

"Which means devil in Portuguese," Frank said. "You couldn't think of a better name for that horrible creature."

Joe yawned. "We've left him far behind. Now it's me for dreamland."

They both were soon sound asleep on the banks of the Amazon. The sun had risen by the time they woke. After breakfasting on bananas and berries, they walked along the shore, waving and shouting at boats passing by in the middle of the river.

"No go," Joe said after a while. "They're too far out to notice us."

"We'll have to build a raft," Frank stated. "There are plenty of fallen trees in the jungle. They'll do for logs."

The boys began hauling tree trunks out of the nearest patch of jungle. When they had gathered about a dozen, Frank lined them up in a row. Joe pulled down some thick, sinuous creepers from the trees to use as rope. Skilfully they braided the creepers over and round the logs. The result was a seaworthy raft. Flat driftwood provided a pair of paddles.

The boys gave their craft a stiff push into deep water. Then they scrambled on to it and began paddling towards the middle of the Amazon.

The strong current caught the raft, propelling it along at a rapid rate. "No use fighting this," Joe panted. "The best we can do is travel on a diagonal line downstream."

Dipping their makeshift paddles rhythmically into the water, the boys managed to guide their raft towards the lanes followed by river traffic.

Frank ceased paddling and looked around at the bare expanse of water, sky, and jungle. "We seem to have the Amazon all to ourselves."

Joe also shipped his paddle. "Well, we're far enough out, Frank. There'll be boats coming by and we'll be able to hitch a ride back to Manaus."

He rose to his feet, shaded his eyes with his hands, and squinted up the river. A dot on the horizon grew larger. The outline of a substantial vessel took shape.

"Tour ship coming," Joe announced jubilantly. "I'll flag it down." Taking off his shirt, he fastened it to his paddle by the cuffs. Then he began to wave his improvised flag at the ship, which slowed down and eased alongside.

A rope ladder swung down over the railing. The boys quickly mounted to the deck. In the captain's cabin, they told him that they had become lost in the jungle on the previous night.

"Where do you wish to go?" the captain asked.

"To Manaus," Frank answered.

"We will be glad to take you."

"Thank you very much, sir."

Frank and Joe freshened up and had a second breakfast. "Good thing we've still got our money," Frank said with a grin. "It got soaked, but it'll still buy us what we need."

"How about a plane trip back to Belem?" Joe asked.

"Good idea. The only thing is, who's going to take us?"

Joe shrugged. "We'll just have to make it to the airport and play it by ear."

It was about noontime when the Hardys arrived in Manaus. After getting their bags, they took a taxi to the airfield and Frank inquired if Rico Armand happened to be there.

The airport manager, a rotund Brazilian with a bald head, shrugged. "If you know his plane, go out and look around. There are many small planes coming in here and I do not know all the pilots by name."

The boys made a methodical search of the field.

"Hey, Frank," Joe said, "doesn't that crate look like the one we came on?"

"Sure does. I recognize the number. Wow, are we in luck!"

"Tell you what," Joe said. "I'll stay here by the plane while you try to locate Armand."

"Okay." Frank left. He returned a half hour later without the pilot. "Somebody told me he'd be flying out about three o'clock," he said. "But no one knows where he is now."

"We'll wait right here," Joe said. "It's our best bet."

The boys squatted down beside a hangar from where they could keep the plane under surveillance. Rico Armand appeared about a half hour later. He was surprised to see the boys, who quickly asked for a ride back to Belem.

"Sure, get in," the pilot said. "I'll be glad to take you."

They arrived in Belem in the evening and found a

small hotel to spend the night. After dinner they discussed the situation.

"What next?" Joe asked, stifling a yawn.

"Obviously the Brazilian angle was nothing but a wild-goose chase," Frank said. "We were lured here by San Marten and his gang to be eliminated."

"Suppose Retson had come instead of sending us?"

"Then no doubt he would have run into the same difficulties."

"Too bad we didn't learn where Graham really is," Joe said with a sigh.

"Back north most likely meant the United States. I vote we return to Granite City and work on the case from there," Frank said.

"I'm with you. Maybe we can get our papers tomorrow."

At the American Consulate the next day the Hardys were greeted by the same man they had spoken to before. "Your passport problem is solved," he told them. "The lost ones have been cancelled. Here are a couple of identification cards that will enable you to return home."

"Thank you, sir," Frank replied.

The young detectives made plane reservations and sent a cable to their family, saying they would be on a late-afternoon flight from Belem to New York. Then they taxied to the airport, bought tickets, and boarded a jet.

Before they left the ground, Joe, who was at the window, nudged his brother. "Frank, look at that!"

They saw a crate with a howler monkey being lifted into the hold of a plane operated by another airline The animal stood on its hind legs, grasping the bars, and peered through with sharp black eyes.

"Would you say that's Diabo?" Joe asked.

"Hardly. This one has a pleasant face, not at all like the leering monster we tangled with."

They landed at Kennedy Airport the following morning. After they made their way through customs, they found Chet Morton waiting for them with a big grin.

Joe clapped their freckle-faced friend on the shoulder. "Chet, how did you know we were coming?"

"I had something to do for my dad in New York. Before I left, your mother called me. She got your cable and asked me to let you know your father's coming in on the shuttle from Washington just about now. He'll join us for the connecting flight to Bayport."

The three youths went to the shuttle terminal coffee shop to kill time while waiting for Fenton Hardy. They took a booth near a window where they could see the planes coming down for a landing.

After the waitress had served them, Frank sipped his coke. "How's business, Chet? Last we knew Phil and Tony were joining forces with you in the golf ball project."

"Anyone drown in a water hazard yet?" Joe needled their rotund pal.

Chet downed a bite of doughnut. "You guys don't take scavenging seriously enough," he said. "Business is booming. We've recovered about a thousand balls. At least a hundred bucks apiece for each of us."

Frank brought the conversation round to the mystery. "Chet, what's going on in Whisperwood? Everything quiet out there?"

"Quiet!" Chet exclaimed. "Are you kidding? Mrs

Retson had completely disappeared!"

Frank drew a sharp breath. "Disappeared!" he repeated incredulously.

"Gone! Scrammed! Vamoosed!" Chet replied.

"Give us the facts," Joe said grimly.

"First I learned about it was when I went up to the house the day after you left. Mr Retson blew his top. Told me his wife had vanished from her room."

"What about Hopkins the nurse?" Frank put in. "She must have been on duty."

"Says she heard nothing. She was eating her lunch in another room. When she returned, she found the bed empty. She's been having hysterics. Claims you two upset Mrs Retson so much she just up and ran away."

"So we have two mysteries," Frank said. "First it was Graham, now it's his mother."

"There must be some connection," Joe observed. "I'll bet San Marten is behind this too."

"Maybe Mrs Retson received a secret message from Graham," Chet ventured. "He might have let her know somehow where she could find him."

"It's possible," Frank replied. "Joe and I failed to locate Graham in Brazil." He told Chet about their trip.

Suddenly Chet said, "Do you know a guy who wears a Panama hat?"

Frank shook his head. "I can't think of anyone."

"Me either," Joe chimed in. "Why?"

"There's a man standing in the doorway who seems awfully interested in you!"

·11·

Dangerous Stranger

JOE casually turned round for a look. The doorway was empty!

"Whoever it was, he's gone," Joe said.

"Well, he sure gave you fellows the once-over," Chet stated. "Kept staring at you as if you were his long-lost cousins."

A sudden thought caused Joe to sit bolt upright. "What if this character followed us from Belem, Frank! Maybe it was San Marten!"

"What did the man in the Panama hat look like?" Frank asked.

"Small, scrawny. Has blond sideburns. Wears steel-rimmed spectacles."

Joe breathed a sigh of relief. "It wasn't San Marten, thank goodness."

"Could be one of his gang," Frank stated. "On the other hand, maybe the man thought we were somebody else and realized his mistake."

"Well, I watched him for a while to make sure," Chet said. "He never took his eyes off this booth till Joe turned round."

"Listen, they're announcing Dad's plane," Frank said.

Joe nodded. "Let's go outside and meet him."

The boys quickly paid their check and went to the gate. The detective came through shortly and shook hands with all of them.

"How much time do we have before our flight leaves for Bayport?" he asked.

"An hour, Dad," Joe replied.

"Then let's park ourselves somewhere and compare notes about our investigations."

"Okay, Dad," Frank said.

They went to the airline waiting room, where they settled themselves in easy chairs round a low table. Mr Hardy kept a firm grip on his black briefcase.

"This is loaded with vital documents," he said in an undertone. "I'd be in big trouble if a thief grabbed it and got away."

"Have you had any breaks in your investigation of the passport gang?" Joe asked.

"Yes. A man carrying one of the stolen and doctored passports was apprehended at Kennedy Airport."

Chet looked glum. "Then there's nothing for us to do, Mr Hardy. You solved the case without us."

The Bayport detective smiled. "Not quite, Chet. Our suspect clammed up. I'll have to run down more clues before I collar the ringleader. You fellows and your pals may come in handy before we round up the gang. By the way," he continued, "how's your own case progressing? Have you found Graham Retson?"

-Frank described their fruitless quest for Graham in Brazil and Joe told about San Marten's attempts to eliminate them, including an account of the hideous Diabo.

Mr Hardy frowned. "I didn't think the Retson case

was going to be that dangerous," he said, sounding worried.

"That isn't all, Dad," Joe went on. "We haven't found Graham, and now Mrs Retson is missing."

"Come again?"

"Chet can explain. He was there."

Chet repeated the story of how Mrs Retson had vanished from her room.

"As I understand it, Chet, you, Phil and Tony were supposed to keep Whisperwood under surveillance," Mr Hardy said mildly.

"Correct, sir," Chet said. "But we were out golf ball scavenging when Mrs Retson got away."

A voice over the loudspeaker announced that the plane for Bayport was ready to board. Gripping his briefcase firmly under his left arm, Mr Hardy led the way to the ramp. Once on board, he retired to the back of the lightly loaded plane to examine some papers. Frank and Chet took two seats together, while Joe sat in the same row across the aisle. There was nobody behind them. Only a few passengers were scattered around the rest of the cabin, and several went to sleep as soon as the plane became airborne.

Chet unbuckled his seat belt and returned to the subject of golf balls. "You want to know the system I've worked out so we don't miss any?" he asked.

"Sure," Frank said.

"Well, Phil and Tony work as my divers."

"What do you need them for? I thought the suction pump did the trick," Joe said.

"It does, in most cases. But some of the water-holes and lakes are too deep and my hose doesn't reach down. So I hold a large basket on a long rope and let Phil and

Tony fill it up. We've brought back quite a haul every time."

"And that way *you* don't get wet," Frank noted.

Chet assumed a hurt look. "You guys know me better than that. I'm the brains of the operation. I've got to direct traffic topside."

Frank and Joe kept needling their pal. Suddenly he jarred them by saying, "Something mysterious is going on at the Olympic Health Club!"

"I thought you couldn't get a contract there," Joe said. "How did you get in?"

"Oh, I didn't," Chet admitted. "But I have an agreement with the golf course next door. During the night I saw strange things over at the Olympic. So did Phil and Tony. They'll back me up."

"What kind of strange things, Chet?" Frank asked.

"Flickering lights on the roof. They flashed on and off, then went out for good. We never saw that happen before. Couldn't figure out what it meant."

"Was that all?" Joe inquired.

"No. There were peculiar noises, too. Like someone shouting. At first I thought I was hearing things. But when Phil and Tony came up from their dive, they heard it too."

"Did you investigate?"

"We climbed over the fence and sneaked into the golf course. But whoever was there had gone by the time we made it."

As the boys talked, Fenton Hardy looked up from his papers. He noticed a man rise and walk slowly down the aisle. The passenger then eased himself into a seat behind Frank and Chet, who never noticed him.

Sensing something sinister about the man, Mr

Hardy strode down the aisle and paused to observe the stranger a few steps to the rear.

Covertly the man drew something from his pocket. Shielding his hands with his body, he fiddled with the object until a metallic clicking sound occurred. He hunched over, feeling for the space between the seats in front of him, where Frank and Chet sat. With the other hand he guided a long slender tube into the space.

"Just a minute!" Fenton Hardy said sternly. He grabbed the man by the collar and hauled him out into the aisle. As he did, the plane hit some turbulence, jostling the passengers. Fenton Hardy was thrown to one side. The other man fell to the floor heavily, with the tube under his hand. He lost consciousness!

A stewardess ran up to inquire what was wrong. "This!" said the detective. He picked up the tube, which had a sharp needle projecting from one end. "It punctured his wrist," Mr Hardy went on. "It might be poison. He needs a doctor."

The pilot radioed ahead, then made an emergency landing at an airport near a small town. An ambulance rushed the stricken man to a hospital while Fenton Hardy and the three boys followed behind in a police car.

In the emergency room an intern examined the stricken passenger and the tube, then administered an injection.

"Was it poison?" Fenton Hardy asked.

"Yes. Definitely. The antidote seems to be working, although he nearly died. Who is this man?"

The officer went through the victim's pockets. When he pulled out a United States passport, Mr Hardy asked to see it. It was issued to Harold Solomon.

"It's not genuine," the detective said.

"How do you know?" the officer asked.

"It's my business to know," Mr Hardy replied, and showed his credentials to the policeman.

"Then we'll hold Solomon on several charges," the officer said. "Attempted murder and carrying a false passport."

Frank, Joe and Chet, meanwhile, discussed the bizarre case. "A poisoned needle!" Frank shuddered. "And it was meant for us!"

Chet walked over and looked at the ashen face of the stranger, who was still unconscious. "You want to know something!" he said suddenly. "That's the guy who was watching you in New York!"

·12·

The Monkey Mask

THE boys peered down at Solomon, whose eyelids began to flutter.

"He must belong to San Marten's gang," Joe said. "Probably a professional killer."

"That's a good theory," Fenton Hardy agreed. "I've checked his clothing. No identification marks. But his suit, shoes, and hat are all South American style. I'd say he's from Brazil. But here's the clincher."

The detective held a ticket between his fingers.

"What's that?" Joe asked.

"A baggage claim check for a crate back at Kennedy Airport. Guess what's in the crate!"

Joe gasped as the truth suddenly dawned on him. "A monkey!"

"Right. The claim check is clipped to a health certificate declaring the animal has had all its shots and can be brought into the United States."

Two more policemen, one a captain, entered the hospital as he was speaking. Introductions were made. "Good to meet you, Mr Hardy," the captain said. "We can always use an assist from America's number one private eye."

"Thanks for the compliment," the detective replied.

"But the praise actually belongs to these young men. They can tell you what happened."

Frank described the trip to Brazil. Then Chet reported how the man in the Panama hat had kept them under surveillance at Kennedy Airport. Joe explained his theory that the man belonged to San Marten's gang.

"That seems to make sense," the captain said. "We're here to take Solomon into custody—if that's really who he is. He's conscious now. All of you can come along and hear what he has to say for himself. We've examined the plane, by the way. It's clean."

The doctor said the patient was well enough to leave the hospital. Two squad cars took the group to headquarters.

After the prisoner was seated and given a drink of water, he was advised of his rights to consult a lawyer before answering questions. He nodded and even refused to divulge his name.

"It really isn't Solomon, is it?" the captain asked. "And what's your nationality?"

"None of your business."

"Where did you get the metal tube with the poisoned needle?"

"It isn't mine. I happened to fall on it in the aisle. And I won't have any more to say until I see a lawyer."

"That's your privilege," the officer replied.

The prisoner was taken to a cell. Fenton Hardy summoned the three youths aside for a conference on their next move.

"I'll stay here to press charges against Solomon," he said. "What plans do you have?"

Frank made a quick decision. "I think we should go

back to New York with that baggage claim check. The crate calls for a look-see."

"That's what I had in mind, too," Joe agreed.

The police provided photographs of the ticket claim check and the health certificate and kept the originals for evidence.

"I'll continue on to Bayport," Chet remarked. "I'll brief the folks back home on the latest news from the Hardys, and then hit the road for Granite City."

The group broke up. Frank and Joe returned to the airfield with Chet, and soon everyone was airborne.

Frank and Joe had lunch aboard the plane. Upon landing at Kennedy they hastened to the warehouse where the animals in transit were kept. They told the attendant that a friend had supplied them with the photographs and asked them to take a look at the monkey. He would pick the animal up later. The man told the boys to follow him and led the way through the building.

It was an enormous structure lined with cages of many sizes.

"This must be how Noah's Ark looked," Joe said as they walked along. "I've already counted a baby hippo, a pair of lions, a sackful of snakes, and a wild assortment of zebras, tapirs, and antelopes."

"Not to mention plain old cats and dogs," Frank said with a grin. "Who owns these animals?" he asked the attendant.

"Well," the man replied, "the domestic animals are mostly pets belonging to passengers. The rest are bound for zoos, menageries, and circuses."

"San Marten's line," Joe muttered to Frank. "He told us he was a wild animal trader. Remember?"

"Yes. But that obviously was a cover-up."

Suddenly another attendant came dashing through the warehouse. "A snake has gotten loose!" he yelled. "A king cobra!"

The Hardys knew that cobra venom was among the deadliest of all. And the king cobra was the biggest of the poisonous serpents, reaching a length of twelve feet or more!

"Where is it now?" asked the first attendant.

"I don't know. I found the lid to its box ajar. It slipped out unnoticed. Goodness knows where it is!"

"Okay, everybody be careful," the other man warned. "Don't step into a dark patch on the floor without looking to see if it moves. And don't feel around the tops of the cages with your hand. This cobra could be lurking anywhere. And it strikes like greased lightning."

"We'd like to help capture the cobra," Frank offered. "We've had experience with them."

"Fine. Let's spread out and go over this warehouse yard by yard. First one to spot it, sing out loud and clear."

Joe moved to the area housing the birds. In one cage an Andes condor flapped its wings. A dozen brilliantly hued parrots lent a splash of colour to the dim interior of the place. Some jungle fowl began to cluck and scold.

Joe edged towards them. A slithering movement behind him caused him to turn. Around the corner of the cage whipped a king cobra at least twelve feet long!

It reared three feet off the floor. The hood spread wide open, and the reptile began to sway slowly from side to side. Its eyes locked on to Joe's with a malevolent stare.

Sweat poured down the boy's face. His hands felt clammy. "It's too close to miss me," he thought.

For what seemed like an eternity, Joe stood as immobile as a statue. If he turned to run, the cobra would strike. The fangs would pierce his leg, pumping venom into his blood stream that would cause him to die in agony. Joe's nerves started to give way. He would have to move!

Suddenly a cord dropped over the serpent's head, pulling it to one side. Frank stood there holding the creature securely in the loop of a snake hunter's rod. The cobra writhed and twisted, hissing ferociously, but it could not break the hold of the loop. Skilfully Frank manoeuvred the snake over to its box, dropped it in, and slammed the lid.

Trembling from head to foot, Joe sat down on the next cage. He was too shaken to speak.

"Take it easy," Frank advised. "When I heard the jungle fowl clucking, I figured they were scared of something. So I hustled over for a look. But I didn't expect to see you cornered by the runaway snake."

Frank gave Joe a minute to rest. Then they went to the cage corresponding to the number on the baggage claim check. Inside sat a howler monkey. He looked like the one they had seen at the Belem airport!

He chattered and gazed at them with a gentle demeanour, holding out one paw appealingly as if to shake hands.

Frank rubbed his chin. "We thought this critter was too nice to be Diabo. We were right, weren't we?"

"Absolutely. I'll never forget the way Diabo snapped at us. This is an amiable monkey. Must be from a better jungle family."

The boys turned to leave. As they neared the door on their way out, two men walked in. One was dressed in a whipcord jacket and corduroy pants. The other had on a trench coat and a snap-brim hat. Their faces were hard. They beckoned to the attendant, who was walking a few steps ahead of the Hardys.

"We came to get a monkey you have here," Corduroy Pants said.

"May I see your claim check?"

"Forget it, buddy," Snap-brim growled. "We lost it. But we know the number. That's good enough for us. It's good enough for you."

As the attendant eyed the intruders nervously, Frank pulled Joe behind a cage with baby hippos.

"What's the number?" the warehouse man asked.

"Forty-two-o-seven-six."

The attendant led the way back to the cage he had shown the Hardys.

"I'll have to call the supervisor," he told the men. "I'm not allowed to give you the monkey without a claim check."

"That's all right," Snap-brim said. "Meanwhile we'll go see our little pet."

"Did you send your friends to look at the monkey?" the attendant asked timidly.

"What?" Snap-brim looked puzzled.

"Never mind," Corduroy Pants said impatiently. "Call the supervisor. We're in a hurry."

As soon as the attendant had left, the two men grasped the cage by the corners. Grunting and swearing, they manoeuvred it out of the warehouse as fast as they could to a station wagon parked nearby.

Frank and Joe, ducking behind crates, had trailed

the two men to the spot where the monkey cage had stood, then followed them to the door. They saw Snap-brim and Corduroy Pants lifting the cage into the rear of the vehicle.

As they did, the cage tilted and a package wrapped in brown paper fell out on to the road. The men did not see it. They hopped into the car and drove off.

"We've got to follow them!" Frank said. The boys ran out of the warehouse. Joe pounced on the package, which was small enough for him to slip into his jacket pocket. Frank took down the licence number of the men's car, at the same time flagging a taxi. The boys jumped in, and Frank ordered the driver to follow the station wagon.

It moved fast in the heavy traffic at the airport. The driver kept right on its tail, zooming round and past slower cars. It was a close race until the station wagon whizzed through a red light.

The taxi had to stop. Disappointed, the boys watched their quarry vanish into the myriad of cars headed for New York City.

"No use trying to catch up with them now," Frank said, and told the driver to return to the airport. They got out and paid the fare.

Joe suddenly remembered the package he had picked up. "Let's see what is in it," he said. "Maybe it'll give us an idea of what to do next."

He unwrapped the brown paper and took out a rubber mask of a hideous countenance. The snout was misshapen. The eyes were mere slits of hatred. The fangs were bared in a savage scowl!

"A monkey mask! It's the face of Diabo!" Joe exclaimed.

·13·

One More Chance

"THE face of Diabo!" Frank repeated. "Now I get it. This hideous mask is a form of pyschological warfare. It sure can scare the wits out of a victim."

Joe turned the mask over, noting how the rubber would stretch under a simian's jaw and over the back of its head. The earpieces were broad and thick, almost like earmuffs.

"Do you suppose," Frank said, "that the monkey in the cage really was Diabo?"

"That howler was friendly," Joe replied. "I can't imagine him spitting and snarling like Diabo."

Frank snapped his fingers. "Joe, something else just occurred to me. If San Marten knows this fellow Solomon, then the Brazilian may be involved in Dad's passport case, too! Remember, Solomon had a doctored passport."

"Wow!" Joe shook his head. "This San Marten is really a master criminal. Playing two rackets at the same time."

"Except that we don't know for sure that the monkey is Diabo."

"I can't believe he is," Joe said. "But it would be a strange coincidence if he wasn't."

98

Frank and Joe took a plane back to Bayport. At home they held a long session with their father after dinner.

"I go along with your suspicion of San Marten as far as the passport racket is concerned," Mr Hardy said. "The man's an enigma. The Brazilian Embassy hasn't been able to come up with any information on him. All they know is that he lives in Belem, has no police record down there, and doesn't court publicity."

"Anyhow, maybe we can help each other in our investigations," Frank said.

"Right. If I smash the passport gang, it may lead me to Graham Retson. Or, if you fellows find Graham, you may find the gang's ringleader at the same time."

Early the next morning Frank and Joe drove back to Whisperwood to join their buddies. Chet was in high spirits. "I hope you guys are doing as well as we are," he greeted them.

"Just how well is that?" Joe asked.

"We retrieved a couple of hundred more golf balls last night," Phil said.

"Most of them in pretty good condition, too," Tony added. "They'll bring in a lot of clams after we put them in the washing machine."

"Tonight," Chet said, "we'll be working the big water-hole at the Olympic Health Club."

"I thought they wouldn't give you a contract," Frank put in.

Phil winked. "They wouldn't let Chet in the place. But Tony and I wangled the contract."

"It was easy," Tony said. "We just walked in and said how about it and they said okay."

"Wait a minute," Chet interrupted. "You guys were my bird dogs. I let you go ahead, that was all. I could have made the deal if I had wanted to."

When the boys' laughter at his bragging had subsided, Frank and Joe asked Chet about Mrs Retson. They were told she was still missing. The Hardys went to the mansion to report to their client. Harris opened the door.

"Mr Retson is in the den," he said and escorted them in.

Retson was seated at his desk, looking over some papers. He glanced up in surprise.

"Hello, Mr Retson," said Frank. "We're sorry to hear about your wife."

"What? Oh yes. More trouble. All I seem to have is trouble. Well, where's Graham?"

"I'm afraid we haven't found him," Frank said. He explained about San Marten and the wild-goose chase up the Amazon.

"So you failed!" Retson exploded. "I should have known this case was too big for a couple of amateurs!"

"Sir, we haven't failed completely," Frank said coolly. "We have reason to believe that your son was kidnapped. Chances are he is somewhere in the United States."

"And is being held captive by San Marten and his gang," Joe added.

"Nonsense!" Retson said. "I don't believe there's any such person as this San Marten you keep talking about."

Retson composed himself and in a lower voice added, "I'll give you one more chance. But if you don't find my son pronto, you're fired."

"Mr Retson, have the police investigated the disappearance of your wife?" Frank asked.

"Yes, yes. They're working on it. You don't have to concern yourself with that."

"She and Graham might have been kidnapped by the gang!" Joe put in.

"I doubt it," Retson said sharply. "A rope ladder was found hanging down from her window. I believe she completely lost her mind and ran away. You leave that up to the police. Just find Graham!"

The Hardys returned to the guesthouse. On the way Joe said, "Retson brushed off his wife's disappearance quite casually."

"He sure did," Frank agreed. "And he doesn't seem to take us very seriously, either."

"We'll have to do something to convince him that he can rely on us," Joe said. "But what? We haven't got a single clue to go on."

"Let's try the Olympic Health Club," Frank said. "Those flickering lights and the noises Chet reported might mean something. Also, remember the Condor golf ball which was thrown into our window the first night? That points to the Olympic too, according to Chet."

Joe nodded. "Let's join the scavenging operation tonight and check out the premises. Another thing. What should we do about Mrs Retson?"

"Nothing. I'm sure once we find Graham, we'll find his mother."

Chet was enthusiastic when he heard that the Hardys would join him that night. "We can use all the help we can get. We'll even cut you in on the profits!" he said with a grin.

During the rest of the day, Frank and Joe kept the mansion and the staff under surveillance, but nothing unusual happened. At nightfall the five boys drove to the club in Chet's pick-up with the suction pump in the back. The Olympic golf pro, Gus McCormick, let them in, waited while they transferred the pump to a golf cart, and watched them vanish into the darkness over the golf links. Frank wheeled the cart up to the edge of the water-hole, which was a distance from the clubhouse.

"This is a combined operations strategy," Chet said pompously. "We'll have four units acting under central control."

"Where's central control?" Joe asked.

Chet slapped his chest. "Here!"

"Shall we synchronize our watches?" Phil asked jokingly. "Oh, I forgot. I don't have any."

"Neither do I," Tony said. "I won't be able to tell the time when I'm in the pond."

"I'll keep time for all of us," Chet told them.

"Where do Frank and I come in, General?" Joe asked.

"Frank, you handle the hose to the suction pump. Sweep up all the balls along the edge. Joe, you take the basket and gather the booty that Phil and Tony bring back from the water-hole. Let's go, team!"

By midnight the boys had a basketful of golf balls, and the suction pump container was loaded.

"All right, time to go," Chet said. "We've gathered all the wealth in this place. Those balls in Joe's basket look pretty good to me. Let's take a gander at the container. It'll probably have to be cleaned out."

He lifted the lid, took a peek, gave a low whistle and called, "Hey, fellows, look at what we dredged up tonight!"

Reaching in, he brought out a woman's shoe.

Tony chuckled. "Some lady player must have gone back to the clubhouse barefoot."

"That's not all," Chet said, reaching into the container again. This time he came up with a badly rusted pistol. The other boys looked in amazement.

But before anyone could comment, a loud cry echoed over the golf course. Lights flickered on the clubhouse roof!

·14·

Big Deal for Chet

"THOSE lights must be a signal to somebody!" Joe said excitedly. "Let's get over to the clubhouse and see what's going on!"

Frank grabbed his arm. "Take it easy. Somebody's coming."

The Hardys slipped away into the darkness just as several men ran up to the water-hole. "What are you doing here?" one of them shouted.

Chet explained.

"Who gave you permission?"

"Gus McCormick."

"We have a contract with Gus," Phil said. "We get half the golf balls we retrieve, and he gets half. It's a fifty-fifty deal."

The man grunted angrily. "Well, the deal's off. Gus had no business making it. Now, you three, get out of here. And don't come back or I'll make it hot for you!"

He and his companions strode off towards the clubhouse and the Hardys moved back to the water-hole.

"Those roughnecks are really mad about something," Frank said. "I wonder what's bugging them."

"Beats me," Chet replied. "All the other pros gave us

104

the go-ahead without any beefing by the management. What's so special about this place?"

"Gus acted as if he were in charge," Phil commented. "He was glad to let us do all the work while he was getting half the profits."

"Something fishy's going on," Frank declared. "Remember the shout we heard? And the flickering lights? And the pistol we dredged up?"

"What'll we do now?" Chet asked.

"We'll have to get off the premises," Joe replied. "Let's go back to Whisperwood."

"And we'll contact the authorities tomorrow," Frank added. "Chief Carton might want to take a look at that gun we found."

The Hardys drove into Granite City early in the morning, taking the pistol and the shoe with them. They found the chief at his desk and explained their reason for calling on him.

Carton toyed with a pencil. "I haven't been out to the Olympic Health Club often," he said. "It's a private outfit and no member has turned up on the police blotter yet. However, this pistol calls for an investigation. I'll have it put through tests in our crime lab. Want to come along and watch?"

"Sure would," Joe said, and told the chief about their own private lab at home.

The fingerprint expert could find no prints on the pistol, but the serial number became visible after the weapon had been carefully scraped. Also, it was still in good enough condition to be fired by the ballistics expert, who returned a while later to the lab with his report.

Carton left the office and returned with a file folder.

Then he placed the ballistics report and the open file side by side. He rubbed his chin and commented, "This is very interesting."

"What, sir?" Frank asked.

"A man held up a post office in Granite City two years ago. His name was Roscoe Matthews. This is our file on him." He tapped the folder. Then he hefted the weapon in the palm of his hand. "And this is the holdup gun!"

"Are you sure?"

"The serial number proves it belongs to Matthews. And a bullet found at the crime scene matches the one just fired in our lab."

"Is Matthews a dangerous criminal?" Joe wanted to know.

"Highly so. During the robbery he shot a guard in the shoulder. He would have killed him except the guard's badge deflected the bullet. We put out an all-points bulletin on Matthews, but he dropped out of sight."

A sudden thought struck Joe. "What kind of loot did Matthews get away with?"

"That's the strange thing," Carton answered. "He ignored the money. All he took was a batch of passports."

"Passports!" Frank exclaimed. "That's what our dad is working on right now!" He gave Carton a quick explanation of both their father's case and their own.

"Do you have a picture of Matthews?" Joe asked.

Carton pulled a photograph out of the file. It showed a broad-faced blond man with a long nose and a slight squint. It was not San Marten, as Joe had secretly hoped, and Carton had no further information to give.

"Was Matthews a member of the Olympic Health Club?" Frank asked.

Carton shook his head. "No. How the gun ever got into their water-hole is a mystery to me!"

"Talking about the water-hole," Joe said, "we also found a shoe. It probably doesn't mean anything, but we brought it along anyhow." He pulled the shoe from the paper bag in which he had carried the two items.

Carton looked at it. "All I can say is it hasn't been under water very long."

An idea flashed into Frank's mind. "Maybe it belongs to Mrs Retson!"

"She might have lost it running away," Joe added. "Or—or do you suppose she was murdered?" he said, his face registering shock.

Carton stared at the shoe. "I'll find out if it belongs to her. If it does, we'll have to dredge the water hazard at the Olympic golf course."

On the way back to Whisperwood the boys discussed the latest turn of events. "I sure hope it's not Mrs Retson's shoe," Joe said.

"Chances are it's not," Frank told him. "Any number of women play golf there. And why should she have run across the course? She would have been seen, recognized, and brought back. Don't forget, she left in bright daylight."

"The question is, did she go on her own or was she kidnapped," Joe mused.

"We've got to zero in on the Olympic Health Club fast, Frank. All these mysteries may be part of one big package."

Back at the guesthouse, the Hardys found Phil and Tony preparing to leave for Bayport.

"What's up?" Joe asked.

"We've picked the golf courses clean around here," Phil answered. "Now we'll give the duffers a chance to dunk some more, then we'll come back for another scavenging operation."

"You're taking off when mysteries are busting out all over," Frank protested.

"We'll be here in a jiffy if you need us," Tony assured him. "Just give the word."

"How about you, Chet?" Joe asked.

Before Chet could reply, the phone rang. He answered, then beckoned Frank and Joe to listen in.

A strange voice asked, "Are you the guy who cleaned out the water-hole at the Olympic Health Club last night?"

"Correct," Chet said.

"Then you're in possession of everything that was dredged up?"

"Correct."

"How would you like to make a fantastic deal for the entire haul?"

"What kind of deal?"

"A cool thousand bucks!"

Chet let out a low whistle. Frank gestured to him to keep the stranger talking.

"That sounds great," Chet went on. "How come—?"

"You wonder why I'm offering so much?" the man interrupted. "Well, I want the golf balls plus everything else your suction pump brought up."

"Like a gun and a shoe?" Chet asked casually.

There was a moment of silence. Then the man said, "I mean everything. Understand?"

"Sure. Will you come over here? Or shall I bring the stuff to your place?"

"Neither. Put it in a golf bag and leave it tonight under the tall elm in the woods south of the Olympic Health Club. Come back tomorrow night, and you'll find your money in a paper bag under the same tree."

The phone clicked off and Chet gulped. "Wow! I'm in the middle of a dangerous mission!" He looked pleadingly at his friends. "I'll need some protection!"

"Don't worry," Frank said.

"I wonder how this guy knew where to find you, Chet," Joe mused.

"That makes the whole business even stickier," Frank replied. "We're on to something big here. Whoever phoned knew the gun was down there, and must be connected with Matthews."

"It could have been Matthews himself," Joe said.

"Who's Matthews?" Chet asked.

Joe told about the ballistics test on the pistol.

"Hey, I'm getting out of here!" Chet quavered. "I don't want to get mixed up with any gunman."

"You'll have to pretend you're going through with the deal," Joe replied. "Besides, there's a thousand bucks in it for you."

"That's what you think! He won't pay!"

Joe grinned. "True. But he won't know if you gave him the gun until he opens the bag. Meanwhile, we can get a look at him."

Swiftly Joe outlined his plan. He took a golf bag from the closet, poured a stream of balls into it, then crumpled up some newspapers and forced them down on top of the balls. Then he lifted the bag in his two hands, testing the weight.

"That's not bad," he said with satisfaction. "Let's hope our plan works."

After lunch Tony and Phil left for Bayport, wishing their friends luck with their case.

"We'll need it," Chet said, apprehensive about their impending mission.

At night the trio drove to the woods near the Olympic Health Club. Frank and Joe circled through the trees, and crouched behind a clump from which they could observe the tall elm. Chet walked openly to the tree. He placed the golf bag upright against the trunk, then went back to the car, got in and waited.

The minutes ticked away. When the moon rose, leaves and branches cast weird shadows on the ground under the elm. In the distance a dog howled.

"My foot's going to sleep," Frank complained in a whisper.

"And I'm getting a backache," Joe replied. "Chet always comes out on the right end of our stakeouts. I imagine he's snoozing comfortably in the car—"

Joe stopped at the sight of a moving shadow. Someone was in the tree.

"Get ready to charge!" Frank advised. "We can't let him escape!"

The figure moved from limb to limb in an agile descent. Bounding to the ground, it turned in the direction of the Hardys, who looked directly into the leering face of Diabo!

Before either of them could move, the simian seized the golf bag and scampered off into the darkness. Pursuit was futile.

"Outwitted by that monkey again!" Joe exploded.

"But he provided a good clue," Frank said. "Old

Diabo is the pet of San Marten, so San Marten is definitely in league with Matthews or his pals. Everything points to the Olympic Health Club as their headquarters!"

"As you always tell me," Joe said wryly, "don't jump to conclusions."

Just then Chet ran up. As Joe had guessed, sleep had overtaken their hefty pal and he had missed the monkey episode.

They drove back to Whisperwood in silence, pondering the odd twist in the case.

At breakfast the next morning the phone rang. The same man was calling Chet.

"Buddy, you pulled a fast one on me last night. But you'd better not try that stunt any more," the man threatened. "You'll hear from me again, and this time make it real or you'll never hunt for another golf ball!"

The phone went dead. Chet looked pale under his freckles. He stretched uncomfortably. "You know," he said, "I'm really not anxious at all to go out of business!"

"You won't," Frank said. "Don't worry. Just sit tight here while we go and check out the Olympic Health Club."

"Okay," Chet said as Frank and Joe left.

At the reception desk of the health club they met Gus McCormick, and told him that they would like to play golf.

"Impossible!" the pro snapped. "It's only for members—the names in here." He slapped the register on the desk.

"Suppose we're the guests of a member?"

"Then it's okay."

"Mind if I have a look at this book?" Frank inquired. "Maybe we know somebody who belongs here."

"Help yourself."

Frank ran his eye down the list of names, while Joe looked over his shoulder. Finally he came to J. G. Retson.

"Can we go in as Mr Retson's guests?" Frank inquired. "We know him quite well."

"He'll have to tell me so himself," said Gus. "Sorry, those are the rules."

"I'll call him." Frank phoned their client, but he was not at home.

"Too bad," said Gus.

"Was Graham Retson a golfer?" Frank asked.

"No. He stuck to table tennis. Usually played with one of our caddies, Harry Grimsel."

"Grimsel? Is he here now?"

"Yeah. In the locker room. Go right through that door if you want to talk to him."

"Thanks."

Frank and Joe went in and found a slim young man putting some golf clubs into a locker. When he turned round, they recognized him. One of the pair in the car they had hit!

·15·

Midnight Pursuit

"H<small>I</small>, Harry!" Joe greeted him. "Long time no see!"

"Remember us?" Frank added. "We met you on the highway."

Grimsel pushed his long hair out of his eyes. "Oh, now I remember," he said. "What can I do for you? Want a game of golf?"

"Maybe later," Joe said. "First we want some information."

"Like what?"

"Does Mr Retson play the Olympic golf course?"

"Yes. I've caddied for him lots of times. He's not much of a player, though. Too hot-tempered. Has a habit of throwing his clubs in the water hazard after a bad shot."

"How well did you know Graham Retson?" Frank inquired.

"Pretty well. We played table tennis together. He talked a lot about himself. Said he couldn't get along with his father and wanted to run away."

"Did he ever tell you where he was planning to go?" Joe asked.

"Well, he mentioned a number of places," the caddy said, knitting his brows as if trying to remember. "The

South Sea Islands, India, Ceylon, Hong Kong, and—"

"Brazil?" Joe interrupted casually.

"No—yes, he did say something about Brazil, but I forget what."

Frank realized that they would not get anything useful out of Grimsel and shrugged. "Maybe he went to the moon. How about some golf now?"

"Okay," the caddy replied. He went off, saying he had to make a phone call first. He returned a few minutes later and supplied the Hardys with clubs and golf balls, then led the way out a side door to the first tee. They each hit a solid drive. Soon there was a putting duel on the green. Frank sank a long putt and took a one-stroke lead.

"Say, you guys play better than most of the club members," Grimsel remarked.

The course wound round the back of the clubhouse. After sinking their shots, Frank and Joe would step aside from a hole and take a good look at it.

"This place is a lot bigger than it looks from the front," Joe muttered to Frank while Grimsel was making his last shot on the ninth hole.

"It seems they've added an entire new wing to the old building," Frank said. "And see that ventilator on top? Must be the biggest unit in Granite City."

On the next hole, Joe stood a few yards to one side as Grimsel started to swing back.

"Do you know anything about howler monkeys, Harry?" Joe asked.

The question broke the flow of the caddy's movement. The ball sliced, struck Joe on the side of the head, and bounded down the fairway.

Joe slumped to the ground as if he had been clubbed

with a bludgeon! Frank rushed to examine him.

"Gosh, I didn't mean to hit him!" Grimsel exclaimed, worried.

Frank looked at the bruise over Joe's left ear.

"I don't think he's badly hurt," he said. "But he's out for the count. We'd better get him back to the clubhouse. You stay here. I'll go for a golf cart."

Frank started off at a run. He was hardly out of sight when Joe stirred. As his eyes focused, he saw Grimsel standing in front of him.

"Sorry I bashed you like that," the caddy said.

"So am I. That's what I get for talking while you concentrated."

"Think you can make it to the clubhouse? Your brother went for a cart, but they all might be in use."

Joe rose to his feet and took a couple of steps. "I'm okay. But what a headache I've got!"

As the two neared the clubhouse they heard loud angry voices. Rounding the corner they found Frank being escorted to the front steps by Gus McCormick. Behind him was a large stout man with a flushed face.

"That's Charles Portner, the general manager," Grimsel whispered.

Portner was furious. "Throw this trespasser off the premises!" he ordered, pointing to Frank. Then he noticed Joe. "Bounce that one, too! He's not a member either. They've got a nerve using our private golf course!"

Portner caught the guilty expression on Grimsel's face. "You didn't give them permission, did you?"

The caddy was silent.

"Answer me!"

"Mr Portner," Harry whined, "I thought it was okay

as long as a member of the staff was with them."

"It wasn't okay. And it won't happen again because you're fired!"

At that moment a police car drove up to the clubhouse. Two officers got out and climbed the steps. "I'm Lieutenant Cain," one of them said. "What's going on here?"

Portner calmed down. "Nothing to bother you with, Lieutenant. Just a couple of trespassers."

"That's your affair," said the other policeman. "We've come on a different matter. Concerns the wife of one of your members."

Portner tucked his chin in and cocked his head. "Who, may I ask?"

"Mrs J. G. Retson. She's disappeared from her home in Whisperwood. We're checking the neighbourhood."

Frank and Joe listened intently as the conversation went on. They quickly realized that the police were being purposely mum about the pistol and the woman's shoe.

"Has Mrs Retson been here at the club recently?" Lieutenant Cain asked.

Portner tapped his forehead. "No. She hasn't been around for at least three months. Of course, I can't swear to it. I might not have seen her."

Portner hesitated, then went on, "A woman has been seen around here several times after nightfall. She ran across the golf course."

"Did anyone recognize her?"

"No."

"Could it have been Mrs Retson?"

Portner frowned. "I have no way of telling. She appeared in the dark, and disappeared in the dark."

"Okay, Mr Portner," said Lieutenant Cain. "We'll continue our search. And let us know if you catch the mysterious lady of the golf links."

As the squad car rolled off down the driveway, the Hardys strolled back to their convertible.

Joe said, "A woman's been running across the golf course. And we've found a woman's shoe at the bottom of the water hazard. How do you figure it?"

"Even if it turns out to be Mrs Retson's shoe, it still doesn't mean she's been murdered," Frank said, trying to cheer both of them up. "Let's give Dad a call when we get to the guesthouse. I think I'd feel better if we could talk it over with him."

Back at Whisperwood, Frank put a call through to Bayport. His mother answered.

"Dad's out of town," she reported. "He's checking some new clues in that passport case. How are you boys?"

Frank decided not to worry her by talking about their latest suspicion. He merely said that they were collecting evidence at the Olympic Health Club.

"A health club sounds safe enough," Laura Hardy said with a soft chuckle. "Stay close to it. And I'll tell Dad you called when I hear from him."

Frank hung up. "We'll take Mother's advice and stick close to the Olympic Health Club. But it may not be as healthy as she thinks!"

That night the boys left Chet in the guesthouse and drove to a road bordering the club. They turned off the lights, parked the car in a stand of trees, and set off for the golf course. At the rear of the clubhouse thick shrubbery provided good cover. They settled down there to keep the place under surveillance.

An hour dragged by. Two. Three. The drone of cicadas lulled Joe to sleep and Frank had trouble keeping his eyes open. Finally they took turns dozing off. Just before dawn headlights flashed into view and two cars turned into the long driveway leading to the clubhouse.

Tensely alert, Frank and Joe crept forward as five men got out. They entered the building and reappeared in a few minutes. One car started off with three passengers. Two men lingered beside the second car and talked in low voices.

"Let's tail this one!" Frank whispered.

They raced across the golf course and climbed into their convertible just as the vehicle came out of the driveway. In total darkness Frank shadowed it, keeping the tail-lights in sight.

The driver ahead sped to the Granite City airport, where he parked near the airstrip. Frank stopped at a distance. Nobody left the waiting car.

"Let's sneak up and spy on them," Joe said.

"Okay." Frank pulled the key from the ignition. Hunched over, they made their way close to the other car. They noticed that only the driver was in it. Obviously the other man had stayed behind at the club.

Suddenly a plane sounded overhead. A small craft came down through the darkness for a landing. It taxied to the edge of the lighted runway and a man stepped out. He hastened to the waiting car and climbed in beside the driver. Who was he?

The boys moved closer and crouched behind a bush near the car. A match flared in the front seat. The newcomer bent forward to touch the flame to his cigarette.

The flickering light played over the man's face. *San Marten!*

·16·

The Ambush

THE match went out, leaving only the burning tip of the cigarette visible in the darkness. San Marten and his friend conversed in low tones.

Frank whispered in Joe's ear, "Let's jump them!"

Joe bolted forward, seized the handle, and flung the door open. He grabbed San Marten by the lapels and started to pull him out when suddenly a powerful spotlight snapped on behind the Hardys, catching them sharply in the white glare.

"We're ambushed!" Frank cried. "Run for it, Joe!"

They turned and ran. San Marten and his companion leaped from the car, and were joined by the man with the light. The three raced after the boys.

In his haste, Joe's foot caught in a vine. He tumbled head over heels, landing on his back. Before he could regain his feet, their pursuers pounced upon him.

Running like mad, Frank was unaware of what had happened until he reached the convertible. Only then did he realize he was alone. He jumped behind the wheel, started the engine, and swung the car around, roaring back to the scene. San Marten and his accomplice had disappeared, and so had Joe. The sound of a motor could be heard in the distance, diminishing gradually in the direction of the highway.

Frank set out in desperate pursuit of Joe and his captors. By the time he reached the highway, the gang's car was out of sight.

Frank made a quick judgment. The Olympic Health Club! "That's where this caper began," he thought. "That's where it will probably end."

He drove to the top of a hill that overlooked the clubhouse. Peering down at the valley, in the first light of day, his eyes followed every turn and twist in the highway for miles ahead. Not a thing moved on the road!

"They must have gone the other way," Frank reasoned. He decided to drive to Granite City and report Joe's capture to the police.

The sergeant at the desk took down the particulars. Frank was turning away, wondering what to do next, when a familiar figure emerged from the office of Police Chief Carton.

"Sam Radley!" Frank exclaimed in amazement. "What are you doing here?"

Fenton Hardy's assistant, a pleasant sandy-haired man, was dressed in a tweed jacket and slacks. He wore heavy shoes and a battered felt hat.

"Hello, Frank," Radley said. "I'm here on a case of my own."

"What's the scoop?"

"Tell you later. First clue me in to what you and Joe are doing."

Frank rapidly described the Retson case, beginning with Graham's disappearance and ending with Joe's kidnapping.

"I'm convinced that we'll find the key to the mystery

in the Olympic Health Club," Frank concluded. "A lot of fishy things have been going on there."

Radley raised his eyebrows and Frank continued, "The general manager seems awfully anxious to keep us away from the place. And now—what about your case?"

Radley rubbed his chin thoughtfully. "When I was in New York a few days ago," he said, "I met an old partner of mine. We used to specialize in missing-person cases. He asked me if I'd undertake an investigation for a good friend of his."

"Who's the good friend, Sam?"

"Mrs Retson of Whisperwood!"

"Mrs Retson!" Frank exclaimed. "And we thought she might be dead. We've been wondering if her body was at the bottom of the Olympic water hazard where we pulled up a woman's shoe and a pistol."

Radley shook his head. "She's in New York in a state of near collapse. Her doctor's keeping her under sedation."

"How did she get there?"

"She climbed out of her bedroom window, caught the bus to New York, and asked her friend to look for Graham. He passed the assignment on to me."

"That's strange," Frank said. "Mrs Retson knew Joe and I were on the case. Why didn't she co-operate with us?"

"Because you're representing her husband."

"What's the difference? They're both looking for their son!"

"That's true. But you're to bring him home. I'm supposed to prevent him from coming home. 'Prevent him at all costs,' was how Mrs Retson put it."

Frank grimaced. "Sam, we're working at cross purposes here."

Radley shook his head again. "Not really, Frank. Mrs Retson thinks her son is in danger. So do you and Joe. Let's rescue Graham and then worry about bringing him home."

Frank started. "What about Joe? We've got to rescue him before we do anything else!"

The sergeant left the desk and approached them. "We've got a tip on that getaway car with your brother," he told Frank. "It was spotted speeding up the road to the abondoned Milten Dairy Farm."

"How do we get there?" Frank asked.

"Take the highway south from Granite City for ten miles. Look for the big Milten sign on the right-hand side. I'll dispatch a car as soon as I can."

Frank and Radley, who carried a small suitcase, hurried out, slid into the convertible, and zoomed down the highway. At the Milten Dairy sign Frank turned off, and the convertible bounced along a rutted dirt road. It led to a complex of barns and sheds.

"Slow down, Frank," Radley said. "There's a car in that big thicket over there."

"It's San Marten's!" Frank replied. He parked behind the thicket, and they got out.

"Look—footprints!" Radley said in a low voice.

The trail led to a run-down house. Carefully the two sleuths edged up to it and peered over a window-sill into a dingy room.

Through the dim light Frank and Sam saw Joe sitting in a chair with his hands tied behind him. San Marten and two other men were taunting the captive with threats.

"You'd be wise to answer my questions," San Marten was saying. "Or I'll let Belkin and Moreno go to work on you. They have ways of making people talk!" He turned to one of the men. "Right, Belkin?"

"You'd better believe it," said Belkin. He pulled out a switchblade knife and tested the edge with his finger. At the same time Moreno turned his face and Frank recognized him. He was the driver of the car the boys had hit alongside the golf course when the sprinkler had obscured their view! Harry Grimsel had been with him.

Joe tugged frantically at the ropes and San Marten clouted him across the face.

As Joe moaned, the door splintered open. Frank and Sam Radley burst in. San Marten and his men spun round, mouths agape.

Frank floored Belkin with a swinging right and fell on top of him. Radley bowled over San Marten and tripped Moreno at the same time!

·17·

Golf Ball Artillery

THE criminals bounded to their feet and a wild mêlée ensued. Punches, karate chops, grunts, and curses filled the room as Joe sat helplessly looking on.

Frank decked San Marten and Radley staggered Moreno with a forearm smash. As Frank and Sam turned to face Belkin, the third member of the gang lifted a chair and knocked both of them to the ground. San Marten pulled himself up shakily.

"Let's go!" he yelled and raced out, followed by his two confederates.

Frank and Sam rose slowly, shaking their heads to clear the cobwebs.

"Thanks," Joe said. "You did a great job."

Frank quickly untied his brother and they dashed towards the big thicket. Radley was the first to spot San Marten's car moving out. It gained speed and disappeared.

The Hardys and Sam jumped into the convertible, eager to take up the pursuit. To Frank's horror the car keys were gone.

"Oh, no! I shouldn't have left them here!" Frank chided himself.

"Don't fret," Sam said. He pulled a pad from his

pocket and wrote something. "I got the licence number. We can phone it to the police."

"Hey, what's that?" Joe said. A glint in the sun had caught his attention. He walked over to it. Nearby in the grass lay the car keys, wet with dew and reflecting the sun's rays.

Frank started the engine and they sped away. At the first public phone booth they stopped and Joe reported to Chief Carton. After a short conversation he told the others that the getaway car had been stolen the day before. "The chief checked the licence number right away. They're on the lookout for it. And another thing—the shoe we found in the water-hole was not Mrs Retson's. Wrong size!"

Frank grinned. "I'm glad about that. Otherwise they might have started dredging the water-hole." As he started the car again, Radley asked Joe:

"What kind of information was San Marten trying to get out of you?"

"He wanted to know about Dad's investigation of the bogus passport ring."

"So he knows Dad's on the case," Frank remarked.

"He sure does. He kept asking where Dad is right now."

"This proves what we suspected," Frank said. "He's in on the passport racket."

"What else did he want to find out?" Radley went on.

"All about Graham Retson. Where is he now? What's he doing? When is he coming home? Things like that."

Frank whistled. "Those were trick questions. We know that he knows where Graham is. He was on a fishing expedition to see how much we've learned."

"That reminds me," Radley said. "How about a bit to eat? There's a restaurant ahead."

"Great idea," Frank agreed. "I'm starved."

Over ham and eggs, they continued to analyse the Retson case.

"We forgot to tell Sam about this," Joe said suddenly and pulled a piece of folded rubber from his pocket.

"The monkey mask!" Frank exclaimed. "How could that have slipped our minds!"

Radley was amazed at Joe's account of Diabo. "This could be very important," he said. "I'd like to take this mask with me. Something tells me it might come in handy before the mystery is solved."

"Where are you going, Sam?"

"To the Olympic Health Club. I called and told them I had arthritis and signed up for the two weeks' treatment they advertise."

"How come you're zooming in on Olympic, too?" Joe wanted to know.

"Mrs Retson is convinced Graham's being held there," Radley revealed. "As a patient, I can do some snooping. See if I can find any trace of him."

"Olympic seems to be San Marten's headquarters," Frank pointed out. "Won't he recognize you?"

"Unlikely," Radley said. "It was pretty dim in that building and he didn't get a chance to see my face. Anyway, it's worth a try."

They got up. "I'd better call a taxi," Sam said. "It would look suspicious if you dropped me off."

When the taxi arrived, Radley got in and waved goodbye.

"Good luck," Frank said, then the Hardys drove on to Whisperwood. Chet was waiting in the guesthouse.

He looked worried and rushed to meet them.

"The guy who played that monkey trick on us called again," he said.

"What did he want this time?" Joe asked.

"His offer of a thousand bucks still stands," Chet replied. "He only wants the pistol."

"What did you say to that?" Frank asked.

"I told him I didn't have it," Chet replied. "But he wouldn't believe me. Said I'll end up in the water-hole myself if I don't deliver the gun."

Frank and Joe agreed it would be safer for Chet if he returned to Bayport right away. They hid behind the suction pump in the back of his pick-up, so they would be on hand if the anonymous caller tried to ambush the truck. They intended to see Chet safely beyond Granite City, planning to return to Whisperwood by bus while their pal continued on home.

Chet was freewheeling the pick-up down a side road towards the highway when a car with two men came racing up behind. He steered to the right, but the other car refused to pass. Instead, the driver cut diagonally into Chet's lane, forcing him off the road into a ditch.

The pick-up truck bucked over a couple of boulders, tilted precariously, and jarred to a halt.

Chet leaped from the cab and ran to the rear of the truck. The two men came after him.

Frank and Joe peered out from their hiding place. *San Marten and Grimsel!*

"Let's see how good my pitching arm is," Frank muttered. Plucking a golf ball from the suction pump container, he took aim and bounced it off San Marten's head.

Joe promptly grabbed a couple of balls and fired

away. Chet quickly leaped on the truck and joined the artillery.

San Marten and Grimsel tried to ward off the barrage with their hands, but the boys kept pitching too fast. Their targets bent over, shielding their heads with their arms.

"Cease fire!" Chet yelled finally. Jumping from the truck, he ploughed into Grimsel with both feet. His weight knocked the caddy into a quivering heap.

Frank and Joe raced after San Marten and subdued him. Quickly they bound his hands with rope from the truck, then tied up Grimsel.

"You'll pay for this!" San Marten snarled.

"Save it for the judge," Frank advised him.

"What'll we do with them now?" Chet asked.

"Take them down to headquarters. Chief Carton will be delighted to see them, no doubt."

The men were lifted into the truck. Frank and Joe stood guard over them, while Chet drove to headquarters. When they arrived, the Hardys announced a citizen's arrest and turned the pair over to be booked.

San Marten and Grimsel were told that it was their constitutional right to consult with a lawyer before making any statements. Then Chief Carton ordered both to be fingerprinted.

At this point San Marten panicked. He resisted the procedure so furiously that it took two officers to hold him while a third cleaned his fingertips preparatory to rolling them in the ink.

The Hardys watched intently. Why would San Marten lose his nerve like this?

"I'll bet he has a record," Frank said to Joe.

San Marten scowled savagely at the Hardys, but he

saw that further resistance was futile. He stood stolidly as his fingers were rolled in the ink and recorded on the FBI standard fingerprint card.

"Send the prints to the FBI," Chief Carton said. "But first check our files to see if we have anything on him."

"Give me a few minutes, Chief," said the officer who had taken the impressions. He left the room.

Carton was discussing the Retson case with the Hardys in his office when the man returned and placed a report on the chief's desk. Carton picked it up, read it, and dropped it with a puzzled frown.

"This is unbelievable!" he said.

·18·

Bad News

FRANK and Joe looked curiously at the police chief. "What's the matter?" Frank asked.

"It doesn't add up," Chief Carton replied. "Here, take a look. Who would you say this is?" He pushed a photograph across the desk. Frank, Joe, and Chet studied it.

"It's Matthews," Joe said. "We saw his picture before."

"That's right," Carton replied.

"What are you getting at?" Frank asked.

"San Marten's fingerprints match those of Roscoe Matthews!"

The boys looked dumbfounded.

"It can't be!" Joe exclaimed. "No two people have exactly the same fingerprints."

"It follows that Matthews and San Marten are the same person!" Frank declared.

He re-examined the photograph of Matthews. "San Marten seems to have a narrower face," he commented.

"And his nose is much shorter," Joe observed.

"Also, no squint," Chet said.

Carton nodded. "San Marten's hair is black, not

blond. Of course that's easy to do with dye. But the other features are so different!"

"Plastic surgery," Frank surmised.

"That's possible," Carton agreed. "It's an old dodge among the criminal elements. Sometimes a crook's mother wouldn't recognize him after the operation." The police chief stared off into space.

"The thing that doesn't fit into this theory is the difference between the behaviour of Matthews and San Marten. Your Brazilian buddy appears to be quite sophisticated and tricky. Matthews wasn't like that at all, according to our records."

"Matthews' personality must have changed along with his face!" Joe said. "It's been done by other criminals."

An idea struck Frank. "Remember Graham Retson's poem, Joe?"

"I sure do."

"What poem?" Carton asked.

"We found it in Graham's room and weren't sure what it meant," Frank said. "It goes like this:

> 'My life is a walled city
> From which I must flee,
> This must my prison be
> So long as I am me.
> There is a way,
> But what it is I cannot say.' "

Carton was thoughtful. "Are you implying Graham Retson wanted to change his identity?"

Frank got up and paced around excitedly. "It sounds far-fetched, but we know San Marten changed his, and Graham is mixed up with San Marten. Isn't it possible that both did the same thing?"

"I don't know," Carton said. "If Graham decided to do this voluntarily, why would San Marten have kidnapped him?"

"I doubt that San Marten would tell us," Joe said. "But maybe Grimsel will volunteer some information."

"Good idea," Carton said, and had the caddy brought in.

He looked frightened. Carton advised him of his constitutional rights, then began to ask him questions. Grimsel answered most of them. Gradually his confidence returned. He even became boastful.

"I know something that could blow the Olympic Health Club wide open," he bragged.

"All right, give us the facts," the chief said.

The caddy smirked. "I'm not that dumb. I know what happens to informers. They end up in the water. Very dead."

"You mean the water hazard on the golf course?" Frank asked in a nonchalant manner.

"Never mind what I mean," Grimsel said surlily. "I'm not talking any more."

Grimsel was taken back to his cell.

"Here's what we do next," Carton said. "We'll get a search warrant for the Olympic Health Club and investigate the place, based on the discovery of the gun."

"We'd like to go along," Frank said.

"Why not? You boys collected most of the evidence so far."

After the warrant was obtained, Chief Carton and two detectives drove to the health club. Frank, Joe, and Chet followed in the pick-up truck. The manager met them as they entered.

"Search warrant, Mr Portner," Chief Carton said

and presented the document for inspection.

Portner turned pale. He examined the warrant briefly, then said, "Go right ahead. We have nothing to hide."

The officers went to inspect the manager's office. Meanwhile, Frank, Joe, and Chet made a tour of the facilities. First they visited the swimming pool, where about twenty members were splashing around. Next they paused in the doorway of the exercise room. Several men were lifting dumbbells and pedalling stationary bikes.

"Nothing suspicious here," Joe said.

Then they went to the gym. Two teams were playing basketball. Another group of four was tossing a medicine ball.

Suddenly Frank felt a thump between his shoulders and pitched forward on his face. The medicine ball had flattened him!

Joe helped him up. Frank was gasping for air.

"Sorry, fellow," a balding man apologized. "My aim isn't usually that bad. I hope you're not hurt."

"Just shaken up," Frank said, and moved on to the steam room with his pals.

Three men were sitting around in thick bath towels, soaking up the heat.

The boys immediately recognized the figure nearest them—Radley! But neither they nor Sam gave a sign that they knew one another.

"Whew!" Radley said to no one in particular. "I could use some ventilation in here!"

Was he trying to give them a hint?

"It's rather hot," Frank agreed. "I don't think I'd like to stay very long."

Sam did not continue the conversation, however, so the boys left. Outside, Frank said in a low voice, "Sam meant to tell us something with that remark. There was no other reason for him to speak."

Joe nodded. "But what did he mean?"

Frank shrugged. "I wish I knew. Just keep it in mind, maybe it'll make sense later."

"Okay. Let's get back and see if the police discovered anything."

They found Portner talking to Carton about Grimsel. "I fired the caddy," said the general manager. "His record here was bad. He broke the rules many times. That's why he's no longer with us."

"Know anything about a man named San Marten?" Carton inquired.

"No."

"A fellow named Matthews?"

"Never heard of him. Really I'm quite unfamiliar with the people you mention. We have so many members and patients who come here for treatment just for short periods that it's impossible to know everyone's name."

The two policemen came back from their search. Carton asked, "Any results?"

"No," one of them replied. "The place appears clean."

Portner looked from one to the other. "At least you could tell me what you were expecting to find?"

"Oh, nothing in particular," the chief replied. "It just so happened that a gun was found in your water hazard which belonged to a fugitive from justice."

"Well, I do hope you're satisfied. I don't want our members disturbed by all this!" The general manager seemed genuinely distressed by the police visit.

"All right, Mr Portner," Carton said. "We'll clear out and let you—"

The phone rang on the desk. Portner answered, then said to Carton, "It's for you."

The officer took the phone. After a brief conversation, he hung up. "Back to headquarters on the double!" he said, his face tense.

As they hurried out to the cars, Frank asked, "What's up?"

"San Marten staged a jailbreak!"

"How did he get away?" Joe asked.

"He had a confederate spring him," the chief replied grimly. He climbed into the squad car.

"You mean another member of his gang?" Frank asked.

"Not on your life!" Carton said. "It wasn't a person at all. San Marten was helped by a monkey!"

·19·

A Telltale Bug

THE news of San Marten's accomplice stunned the Hardys and Chet.

"How did he escape?" Joe asked.

Carton shrugged. "We'll have to wait till we get to headquarters."

The police car drove off, and the boys followed in Chet's pick-up truck. When they arrived, Officer Jensen, who had phoned the chief, supplied the details. "Near as I can figure, the monkey climbed down from the roof, got hold of the bars to San Marten's cell, and wedged himself through. He brought San Marten a plastic explosive and a gun."

"And San Marten did the rest," Joe commented, feelingly.

Jensen nodded. "He planted the explosive under the lock and blew it off. The men on duty came running back to find out what happened. They saw a lot of smoke, dust, and falling plaster."

"Where was San Marten?" Frank asked.

"Under the bed. He scrambled out with the gun in his hand, got the drop on them, and made them throw their gun belts into his cell. Then he locked them in another cell and beat it with the monkey."

"Did the guards get a good look at the animal?" Joe inquired.

Jensen nodded again. "That's one of the strangest things. They said it was the most repulsive creature they've ever seen. A leering, snarling little monster. About three feet high with a long tail and blackish fur."

"Diabo!" Joe gasped.

"What did you say?" Officer Jensen asked with a baffled frown.

"A Brazilian howler monkey we happen to know," Frank said. "Your description fits him perfectly."

Joe explained their experience with Diabo. "We think that horrible face your men saw was a rubber mask."

"A masked monkey! That's a new one on me!" Jensen snorted. "But that was not the only confederate San Marten had when he broke jail. A car was waiting for him outside. San Marten and Diabo jumped in and were gone before we could do anything about it."

"Did Grimsel get away at the same time?" Frank wanted to know.

"No. San Marten left him behind. I've put a special guard on the caddy's cell."

Frank, Joe, and Chet went back to Whisperwood. In the guesthouse Chet slumped into an easy chair. "I'm bushed," he announced. "How about you guys going to the kitchen and rustling up something for the inner man? Make mine milk and ham sandwiches."

Frank chuckled. "Those threatening phone calls don't seem to have affected your appetite, Chet."

"Please, Frank. Don't remind me. Just bring on the eats."

"Okay, okay."

While they were munching on their sandwiches, Joe remarked. "As long as San Marten's still at large, none of us is safe."

"And don't forget the guy who's been phoning me about the pistol found in the water hazard," Chet said. "He's after us, too!"

Joe took a sip of milk. "When we saw Sam in the Olympic steam room, he mentioned the word ventilation. What could he have meant?"

"You know," Frank said, "the ventilation apparatus at the club is huge. Maybe for a reason. I vote we go back tonight and check it out. And it might be a good idea to take some detecting equipment."

"Lucky we've got a spare bugging device," Joe commented. "The other one must have sunk to the bottom of the river when the monkey pushed us into the Amazon."

When it was dark the boys put a scaling ladder and a mountaineer's rope aboard the truck. Then Chet drove to an inconspicuous dirt road and parked in a concealed spot. The three got out, took their gear, and stealthily approached the Olympic Health Club.

The new wing of the club loomed high above. They could barely make out the oblong shape of the ventilator on top.

"We'll have to go all the way up," Frank said in a low tone.

"Not me!" Chet muttered. "I'm volunteering for low-altitude duty."

Joe snickered. "Your weight would probably break the rope. We'll all be better off if you stay below and hold the ladder steady."

They anchored the scaling ladder near some large

bushes. Chet placed his feet against it, and the Hardys climbed the rungs. Frank was first. Joe followed with the rope.

The ladder fell far short of the top. Frank surveyed the gutters and the ventilator, trying to figure out how to get the rest of the way up to the roof. He spotted a two-inch pipe sticking up at one corner of the ventilator.

"That's the hold we need," he thought. Gripping the top rung with one hand, he reached for the rope with the other.

Frank made three tosses before the noose dropped over the pipe. He tested the rope for security, then hoisted himself hand over hand, gaining added leverage by walking up the wall with his feet. Clambering over the gutter, he gestured to Joe to follow.

Joe gripped the rope tightly, then swung himself upward. His feet hit the wall at an angle that caused him to veer wildly away from the building. As he swung back, he felt for the top rung with his right foot, intending to steady himself before making a second attempt to climb up.

His foot probed into empty space! The ladder was gone! Joe dangled at the end of the rope with nothing beneath him except a two-storey drop to the ground!

Desperately he strained every muscle to keep his grip on the rope. Finally he managed to wedge both feet against the wall. Hand over hand, foot by foot, he climbed up until he was high enough for Frank to lean over and haul him on to the roof.

Joe lay there for a moment, gasping for breath.

"What happened to the ladder?" Frank asked.

"We'll have to ask brother Morton about that."

"Come on. Let's take a good look at the ventilator," Frank urged.

Cautiously they crept along the roof until they reached the equipment, which hummed softly. Through an opening they peered far down into a dimly lighted room, far below.

"Let's see if someone's down there," Frank whispered. He removed the listening device from his jacket pocket and lowered the cord into the ventilator shaft. The bug descended and dropped through one of the chinks in a metal grate at the bottom.

Frank held up a hand to indicate that was far enough. He and Joe crouched over the earphones. Sounds came through clearly. A group of men were talking loudly!

"We got the dope on Radley," said one. "He's a fuzz. Works for Fenton Hardy. We'll have to do him in before he sets the Feds on us."

A second voice startled the eavesdroppers. It was San Marten's! "I told you to screen Radley before accepting him for treatment!" he hissed. "Arthritis! What a dodge! And you fell for it!"

"You weren't so quick on the uptake yourself," accused a third voice. "Whose bright idea was it to lure the Hardys to Brazil? Who promised us they'd never come back? We should have knocked them off here in Granite City like I wanted."

The first man spoke again. "Now they have the evidence they need. If they spill what they know, we'll all do time in the pen."

"Stop caterwauling," San Marten commanded. "We can get out of this mess if we keep our heads. I'll devise a new plan."

"I hope it works better than the old one," came a surly reply.

"This one will be foolproof," San Marten promised. "We'll finish off the Hardys and Radley, and get away with the loot. Break it up for now."

Chairs scraped over the floor. The scuffling of feet indicated that the men were rising. Frank motioned Joe to draw the bug up.

"We've heard enough," he whispered. "Let's get away from here and alert Chief Carton!"

"Right," Joe said. "I sure hope Chet's got the ladder up again!" He grasped the cord and pulled on their listening device. It was stuck! He gave the cord a jerk. The bug banged against the metal grating.

"What's that?" San Marten exclaimed.

"Somebody must be spying in the ventilator shaft!"

"Alert Portner and his guards!" San Marten screamed. "And turn the signal lights on. Hurry!"

Lights began to flash on and off at the corners of the roof. Frank and Joe rushed to the parapet, leaving the bug in the shaft. Frank beamed his pocket flashlight. No ladder!

"We'll have to find another way!" Frank ran to the other side of the roof. But there was no alternate escape route in sight!

Suddenly a trap door flew open. Three armed guards sprang out and seized the Hardys at gun-point. They were hustled through the trap door and into a lift for a rapid descent to the room below.

There the lift stopped and the men hurled Frank and Joe out. The boys picked themselves off the floor and were confronted by five men with brutal, cruel, animal-like features.

The men were wearing monkey masks!

"Five oversized Diabos!" Frank said in amazement.

"So you know all about Diabo." The speaker was San Marten. "You're about to meet him again!"

With those words he opened the door of a cage in the corner of the room. Diabo emerged, wearing his hideous mask. The beast looked more sinister than ever because in one paw he held a thin, razor-sharp dagger.

San Marten boomed, "Play your game, Diabo!"

·20·

Unmasking the Gang

THE howler monkey obeyed the command and began a weird caper. He jigged madly round Frank and Joe, waving his arms and throwing his body into contortions. At the same time he rasped out a stream of eerie snarls and whines.

"That's the voodoo dance of the macumba witch doctors!" Frank gasped. "The same as we saw in Belem!"

Diabo circled closer, flailing the stiletto. Another step, and the ferocious simian would be near enough to stab the boys.

Over the monkey's shoulder, Frank and Joe saw a door open. A sixth man slipped into the room. He, too, was wearing a monkey mask. Just as Diabo poised for a thrust at the boys, the sixth man pulled a gun from his pocket.

"Stop!" he shouted.

Startled by the sound, the monkey turned his head. Frank jumped forward and seized the paw that held the dagger. Joe gripped Diabo by the other arm. While the newcomer held the men in check with his gun, Frank and Joe hustled the animal over to the cage, forced him in, and slammed the door.

144

"Thanks," Frank said to their rescuer. "You got here just in time."

"It's a pleasure," came a familiar voice behind the mask. *Sam Radley!*

Sam pulled off his mask. As he did, one of the gang members picked up a small chair and hurled it at him, knocking the gun from his hand. Two men jumped the detective, while the other three went after Frank and Joe.

Frank met the first attacker with a stiff right-hand punch that put him down for the count. Joe felled second with a karate chop. They wrestled the third to the floor, and subdued him after a violent struggle.

Radley took care of his two opponents by grabbing their shirt collars and cracking their heads together. He picked up his gun, and as the gangsters recovered, ordered them to line up along the wall. Sullenly they obeyed.

Then the door opened again. Fenton Hardy rushed in, followed by Chief Carton and a contingent of police. Chet Morton was at their heels.

"Dad!" Frank and Joe cried out in surprise. "How did you get here?"

"I had a late appointment with Chief Carton. A man was caught with a falsified passport in New York, and he spilled the beans regarding the Olympic Health Club. While I was talking to the chief, Chet rushed in and gave us the word."

"Right after you went up on the roof, I heard someone coming so I took the ladder and ducked," Chet said. "Then, before I could set it up again, those lights went on. I was worried plenty, but I see you have the situation here well in hand."

"Sam gets the credit for that," Joe said, and quickly explained to his father what had happened.

"So that's it," Mr Hardy said. "I was wondering how he got in on this caper. You did a great job, Sam."

"You mean your sons did, Fenton," Radley replied. He walked over to the prisoners and began to remove their monkey masks.

"Belkin!" Joe exclaimed as the first face became visible. "The guy who wanted to carve me up with his switchblade knife!"

Radley jerked off the second mask.

"Moreno, our Brazilian buddy's other strong-arm man," Frank told his father.

The third man to be unmasked was San Marten. "No surprise," Joe commented. "We recognized his voice."

When Radley ripped off the fourth mask, the Hardy boys were startled. "Buru!" Frank exclaimed. "What's a Belem witch doctor doing in Granite City? But you're really an American criminal posing as a witch doctor."

Buru's guilty look confirmed Frank's deduction.

Radley reached the end of the line. Putting his fingers under the chin part of the last mask, he wrenched it off. Everyone gasped in amazement. *J. G. Retson!*

"Caught red-handed!" Fenton Hardy declared. "You've got a lot of explaining to do, Mr Retson."

"Wait a minute," said Sam. "There's somebody waiting outside who should be in on this." He went to the door and beckoned. A young man entered. He wore long hair and spectacles that gave him an owlish look. His face was pale.

"Meet Graham Retson," Sam Radley introduced the youth. "He's ready to provide some answers to the questions that have puzzled us in this case."

"Wow!" Joe said, shaking hands with the youth. "We tramped all over Brazil looking for you!"

"Believe me, I wish you had found me sooner," Graham said. "As it was, Sam was just in time to rescue me from the sauna room before I passed out. They locked me in there and turned up the temperature!"

Frank looked at Sam Radley and his father. "How about letting us in on all the details?"

"To begin with," Mr Hardy explained, "San Marten and his gang have been running a Change-Your-Identity operation here at the Olympic Health Club. Criminals were outfitted with new faces, personalities, and passports, which were in ample supply from the post office heist. Of course, the documents were doctored to fit their new owners."

"How did they ever get away with it?" Joe asked. "This health club is a big place, and to keep an operation like this secret—"

"They had everything set up in this room," Radley put in. "It is cleverly concealed from the rest of the building. No one who worked here knew about it, except Portner, Grimsel, and the three musclemen who acted as the ground patrol. Every time those signal lights on the roof flashed on, they checked the premises for unwanted intruders."

With a sidelong glance at San Marten, who stood in silent rage, Carton said, "We've arrested those four already. Grimsel, incidentally, was never really fired. That was just an act Portner put on to underline his 'no trespassers allowed' policy."

"Sam, how did you ever find out about this room?" Frank asked. "We've been here with the police searching the whole place and came up with nothing!"

"It took me a while. It is only accessible by a hidden lift. See that cubicle over there? It's the operating room where the gang's doctor—Buru, incidentally—performed plastic surgery."

"Wow! And we thought he was a witch doctor," Frank said.

"What about personality changes?" Joe asked.

"They brainwashed people," Sam said. "Mostly criminals. For an exorbitant fee they gave them psychiatric treatment, including hypnosis. Moreno here, who poses as a strong-arm man, is really a licensed psychiatrist. Exhibit A—San Marten himself."

Now Graham Retson spoke up. "I learned about their operation by accident. They made me a prisoner in the club."

"You mean you never ran away from home?" Joe asked.

Graham shook his head. "I was going to leave after I found out my father was involved with that gang. I went to the bank and withdrew money, but the bank president notified my father immediately and he intercepted me on my way from the bank to the airport."

Graham paced back and forth as he related the past events. "I tried to escape a few times, but I could never get far enough before they found out. Those lights flashing on and off were signals for the guards to look for me. Once I got as far as Whisperwood—"

"Were you the one who threw a golf ball through the guesthouse window?" Joe interrupted.

"Yes. I thought Harris was there. I didn't know he had moved back into the main house. He was my friend, and I was trying to signal him. My father caught me that time. Another time I almost made it to the waterfall. I heard my mother call me. Then Grimsel and Moreno seemed to appear out of nowhere and Moreno clubbed me. I heard them talking later about Grimsel spotting you at the falls that night."

"So he was the one who pushed me into the water," Frank said.

"Graham," Joe said, "how did your mother know that you were at the Olympic Health Club?"

"I don't think she actually knew for certain. It must have been terrible for her. It caused her breakdown, no doubt. Sam Radley told me about that."

Graham looked at his father accusingly. J. G. Retson flushed.

"I owed money to their loan sharks and couldn't pay it back. So they forced me to work with them. I have many important contacts in industry and was able to launch many of their clients in various businesses. For that the gang charged an extra fee. You discovered the scheme, Graham, so we had to hold you prisoner in the club. I worked out arrangements to send you abroad, however. You would have had your freedom and enough money to live on. Look, Graham—"

"Forget it," Graham said disgustedly.

Frank spoke up. "Why did you insist that we investigate Graham's disappearance, Mr Retson?"

"To make it look good. My wife was suspicious, and I had to convince her that I was eager to find the boy. I didn't want to hurt her, believe me—"

"So you put that note in my jacket to throw suspicion on the butler," Joe cut him short.

"Also," Frank said, "you sent us on that wild-goose

chase to Brazil. You had your nerve, complaining when we returned without Graham!"

Joe turned to Sam Radley. "How did you ever hit on that ventilator clue, Sam"?

"Well," Radley replied, "I had found out about this underground room. But as a patient, I couldn't possibly get down here without being suspect. I figured the only way to investigate was through the ventilator shaft from the outside. I tried it once but almost got caught."

"Not almost," Frank said. "We heard them say that Radley was the fuzz. They knew, and were probably waiting for a good opportunity to get rid of you."

"I guess that just about winds up the case," Fenton Hardy remarked to Chief Carton.

"There's one thing that hasn't been explained yet," Frank spoke up. He went over to the monkey cage. Diabo glared at him through the bars.

"Joe, give me a hand here," Frank said. "I want to see what makes this monkey tick." He opened the door to the cage. Immediately the monkey growled menacingly, and Joe had to use all his might to keep him down while Frank removed the mask.

As soon as the boy had pulled the rubber mask off, the monkey calmed down. A pleasant, gentle simian face emerged, and bright eyes glanced around the gathering in a friendly way. Diabo seemed to be wondering which of these human beings would be good for a handful of nuts or a banana.

Fenton Hardy shook his head in disbelief. "That's the most astonishing transformation I've ever seen," he said. "Diabo must have been trained to be vicious only when he had the mask on. I wonder how."

"Here's a possible answer," Frank said. He turned

the rubber mask inside out, revealing a couple of tiny earphones hidden in the thick earpieces. "Somebody's been radioing instructions to Diabo."

Joe observed San Marten move his head uncomfortably, as if his collar were too tight. The boy went over to examine the prisoner closer.

"Just as I expected!" Joe exclaimed. He removed a collar mike and followed the cord to a sending unit concealed under San Marten's shirt.

The Hardys studied the apparatus. Finally Fenton Hardy said, "I see it now. High-frequency signals sent out between oral instruction could drive the poor animal crazy." He turned to San Marten. "You're a sadist!"

"Dad," Frank said, "I think Diabo's first piece of monkey business was tossing a bag of nuts at me from a truck in Belem."

"Wait a minute, Frank," Joe said. "He wasn't wearing a mask then."

Frank laughed. "You're right. He was strictly monkeying around on his own that time."

"But he had the mask on when he burglarized our room at the hotel," Joe went on.

"And when he pitched us into the Amazon," Frank added.

"Diabo's a very versatile monkey," Chet put in.

"So is the whole gang, in a sinister way," Frank muttered. He was thinking of his first day in Belem. "I wonder if that hotel clerk at the Excelsior Grao Para was in with the gang."

Retson answered. "No. San Marten had someone pose as Graham at the hotel."

"What about Bauer in Manaus?"

"He's a confederate," Retson confirmed.

Frank addressed San Marten. "He was with you that night at the dock when you had us thrown in the Amazon, wasn't he?"

The man shrugged.

"We'll inform the Brazilian police about Bauer," Chief Carton said.

"One more thing," Chet said. "Who phoned me about the pistol?"

"I did," Moreno grumbled.

Chief Carton motioned to his men. "Take the prisoners to headquarters."

Joe Hardy grinned at his brother. "Well, I'm glad that's over. I don't want to do anything more serious than scavenge golf balls with Chet from now on!"

"Count me in, too," said Frank as everyone filed out.

But neither Frank nor Joe were aware that they would have little time to participate in Chet's project. A new case, *The Shattered Helmet*, would soon involve them in a chain of exciting events.

Upstairs in the lobby Frank turned to Graham Retson. "You know," he said, "our first clue in this investigation was a poem we found in your room. It goes like this:

" 'My life is a walled city
    From which I must flee;
    This must my prison be
    So long as—' "

"I remember that," Graham interrupted.

"We figured you were thinking about escaping from home, or even changing your personality when you wrote it. Were we correct in thinking that?"

Graham chuckled. "Sorry, Frank. You were on another wild-goose chase."

"Then what does the poem mean?"

"You'll have to ask the author, not me. I copied it out of a magazine!"

Have you read all the adventures in the "Mystery" series by Enid Blyton?

The Rockingdown Mystery

Roger, Diana, Snubby and Barney hear strange noises in the cellar while staying at Rockingdown Hall. Barney goes to investigate and makes a startling discovery . . .

The Rilloby Fair Mystery

Valuable papers have disappeared – the Green Hands Gang has struck again! Which of Barney's workmates at the circus is responsible? The four friends turn detectives – and have to tackle a dangerous criminal.

The Ring O'Bells Mystery

Eerie things happen at deserted Ring O'Bells Hall – bells start to ring, strange noises are heard in a secret passage, and there are some very unfriendly strangers about. Something very mysterious is going on and the friends mean to find out what . . .

The Rubadub Mystery

Who is the enemy agent at the top-secret submarine harbour? Roger, Diana, Snubby and Barney are determined to find out – and find themselves involved in a most exciting mystery.

The Rat-A-Tat Mystery

When the big knocker on the ancient door of Rat-A-Tat House bangs by itself in the middle of the night, it heralds a series of very peculiar happenings – and provides another action-packed adventure for Roger, Diana, Snubby and Barney.

The Ragamuffin Mystery

"This is going to be the most exciting holiday we've ever had," said Roger – and little does he know how true his words will prove when he and his three friends go to Merlin's Cove and discover the hideout of a gang of thieves.

Armada

GRAIL QUEST

Solo Fantasy Gamebooks

J. H. Brennan

King Arthur's magic realm of Avalon is besieged on every
side by evil powers and foul monsters. You alone can free
the kingdom from its terror, venturing forth on Quests too
deadly for even the bold Knights of the Round Table.
Quests that will lead you to glory — or death.

So sharpen your wits and your trusty sword Excalibur
Junior, and use the intricate combat system to scheme and
fight your way through the adventures in this thrilling
gamebook series. A special score card and detachable
easy-reference rules bookmark are included with each
book.

<table>
<tr><td>The Castle of Darkness</td><td>The Den of Dragons</td></tr>
<tr><td>The Gateway of Doom</td><td>Voyage of Terror</td></tr>
<tr><td>Kingdom of Horror</td><td>Realm of Chaos</td></tr>
<tr><td>Tomb of Nightmares</td><td>Legion of the Dead</td></tr>
</table>

Armada

The Secret Agent's Handbook
A guide for sleuths, spies and privates eyes

PETER ELDIN

Warning!
Before opening this book, make sure the coast is clear. Inside you will find Top Secret Information. Be careful – *it must not fall into the wrong hands*. (And you never know where enemy agents may be lurking.)

Here's the low-down on . . . Coded Messages . . . Secret Handshakes . . . Disguises . . . Passwords . . . Spy Traps . . . Agents' Language . . . Invisible Writing . . . The Toothpaste Hideout . . . and many more highly confidential instructions on how to become a Top Secret Agent.

Top Priority
If you are captured with this handbook in your possession – swallow it!

Another exciting book of fun from Armada

Armada

The Three Investigators

Meet the Three Investigators – brilliant Jupiter Jones, athletic Pete Crenshaw and studious Bob Andrews. Their motto 'We investigate anything' has lead them into some bizarre and dangerous situations. Join the three boys in their sensational mysteries, available only in Armada.

Armada

Nancy Drew Mystery Stories

Nancy Drew is the best-known and most-loved girl detective ever. Join her and her best friends, George Fayne and Bess Marvin, in her many thrilling adventures available in Armada.

Armada

The Hardy Boys Mystery Stories

by Franklin W. Dixon

Have you read all the titles in this exciting mystery series? Look out for these new titles coming in 1987:

No. 41 **The Mysterious Caravan**
No. 42 **Danger on Vampire Trail**
No. 82 **Revenge of the Desert Phantom**
No. 83 **The Skyfire Puzzle**

Armada